AND I LOOKED BACK

AND I LOOKED BACK

EAST ANGLIANS IN THEIR OWN WORDS

GILLIAN CAMPBELL

Matador
Unit E2 Airfield Business Park,
Harrison Road, Market Harborough,
Leicestershire. LE16 7UL
Tel: 0116 279 2299
Email: books@troubador.co.uk
Web: www.troubador.co.uk/matador
Twitter: @matadorbooks

ISBN 978 1803136 905

British Library Cataloguing in Publication Data.
A catalogue record for this book is available from the British Library.

Illustrations by the late John Constable Reeve
by courtesy of his daughter Catherine Orr.

Cover drawing by Harry Becker, in possession of the author.

Printed and bound in the UK by TJ Books Limited, Padstow, Cornwall
Typeset in 12pt Adobe Garamond Pro by Troubador Publishing Ltd, Leicester, UK

Matador is an imprint of Troubador Publishing Ltd

For John

John Constable Reeve was born at Valley Farm, Sproughton in 1929.

A modest man, he was a self-taught artist and at the age of fifteen won his first Founder's Gold Star at the Royal Drawing Society.

Most of his life was spent farming at Mettingham although he continued to paint and built up a reputation for his East Anglian Landscapes and then, due to his connection with the Norfolk & Suffolk Aviation Museum at Flixton, his paintings of 2nd World War aircraft.

He continued painting until his death aged 90 in 2020.

CONTENTS

INTRODUCTION

When I decided to talk to the men and women you will meet in this book it was many years ago and I don't think I had any clear aim other than to make a record of their lives when times were very different before such first-hand recollections were lost. They welcomed me with warmth into their homes and happily re-lived their early years and working lives. Nor had I any idea of the wealth of fascinating memories that they would share. From farmer to fisherman, agricultural engineer to builder, and the youngest housekeeper you could meet, I entered into lives which were by no means ordinary, just going to prove that there is no such thing. The voices you will 'hear', and hear them I'm sure you will, are mainly folk who were firmly grounded in the Waveney Valley in north-east Suffolk, with the occasional 'furrina' from Norfolk. Even though in the early 1990's the changes brought about by computers were a foreign field for most of this older generation during their lifetimes they had already witnessed more rapid changes in our society than they could have ever envisaged when they set out.

The oldest person was May, born in 1891, who lived into her 11th decade from the time of horsedrawn transport to supersonic flight and through two World Wars. The others were born in the early 1900s and they open up for us a period when many had no choice but to leave school as early as 13 years old to find work as soon as possible.

Lives in the countryside were lives of hard work and self-sufficiency following age-old traditions set by the seasons. The magnificent heavy horses, each with their own personalities, that used to work the land were to be slowly replaced by the first tractors. It was a countryside rich in wildlife whose hedgerows were yet to be ripped out; songs of skylarks lifted the spirit and the 'little bit of bread and no cheese' song of the yellowhammer was still to be heard and recognised by town and country children alike.

In most homes a doctor was called upon only when absolutely necessary as he would be an expense people could ill afford. Consequently for everyday ailments they relied on home remedies, many of which would have been passed down through the generations and not all were old wives' tales by any means as some such remedies are still used to this day. Sadly, infectious diseases such as diphtheria and scarlet fever were not uncommon and one or two of these families were left grieving. Another, quite graphic, medical matter may surprise.

The 1st and 2nd World Wars are now relegated to our history books but they had a profound effect on this and following generations. Children grew up in the shadows of those wars, not understanding the ghosts on their fathers' shoulders whose wartime experiences have helped mould who we all are today. Young men such as Sam and Dennis, Harry and John had very different wars. They went off to lands they could only have dreamt of and were to see atrocities which stayed with them for the rest of their lives. One left the gentle Suffolk countryside for the harsh Western Desert; another moved on from trawler to coaster and thence to the Merchant Navy. After five years they must have returned quite different men.

The East Anglian landscape, too, was changed by the wars which brought a welcome boost to the struggling farm economies but they also sped the demise of the shire horses and were a portent of the intensive farming to come. It was not just in the countryside and farming that great changes were beginning; these were the early days of motor cars and how Jack enjoyed them!

Overall we see lives of hard work and simple pleasures, especially for the children, even for Betty whose childhood was cut short by responsibility. There is a tendency to look back to past times with rose-coloured spectacles as if it was a chocolate-box life, but it was no such thing. It was real, it was hard. We should take off those spectacles in order to see a culture now sadly long lost. Each section of the book is devoted to one person or couple. They speak in their own voices, telling their own stories. Where there is dialect I have not attempted to write it as such although the spelling of some words is true to their pronounciation nor have I attempted to punctuate their words as one normally would. They often spoke volubly without punctuation as we all do at times. Their memories may not be entirely accurate but whose two memories of the same event are exactly the same? We cannot bring those times back; there has been a myriad of changes, both good and bad, over the following decades, but it is important that they are not forgotten. Some of their lives were not easy yet there was a sense of contentment with, perhaps, just a touch of nostalgia for the East Anglia they had known. We must listen to the old people. I thank them for sharing their memories.

1

BOB

THE CHEERFUL FARMER

Gordon McDougall, not yet four years of age, was sent to school for the first time with his sister Annie on September 29th 1890. Gordon did not wish to be there, "…he screamed for nearly an hour in passion and there was no pacifying him. He kicked and bit his sister and she cried." So reads the log book of the school's Headmistress. The following day his sister was told to take him home. On October 2nd, "Annie McDougall took her little brother home in the morning and again in the afternoon. He cried and put himself in a frightful passion to get his own way. Told Annie I could not have him at school again. It is plain that by crying and putting himself in a passion he gets his own way." Then on October 10th – "Little Gordon McDougall visited Thursday afternoon, he knocked at the door and I went to it. He was successful in turning over one inkstand and endeavoured to turn over another. Cried for his sister's slate. He is too young to come to school." It was not until April 11th 1892 that Gordon was re-admitted, "He behaved much better than I anticipated he would. Friday he bit Barbara's hand because she went to put his hands together for the Creed. He was put in the corner and stayed there quietly."

Such was life in a small rural school at a time when agriculture was in the doldrums and families were struggling to make ends meet. No doubt little Gordon's mother needed him out of the way so that she could work and, to her, the school mistress was a good enough baby sitter. The Headmistress' diary gives a grim picture of the rural conditions and the ever present poverty endured by the pupils and their families. Small children as young as four had long walks to school, often two or three miles, on bad roads, coping with mud, floods and snow. "Little Frederick Pearson entered in Admission Register, but do not know his age yet. He only came on Monday. He said his legs ached so the next morning; they live rather a long distance from the school and it has been so cold since." Then "Little Smiths have returned after an absence of 9 weeks, they had no boots." As the families led such a hand-to-mouth existence education was not one of their priorities or that of their children. Once the shooting season was underway a good number of boys played truant as they were enticed to go brushing for a small sum. In June one boy was away for over a week working at the Hall catching caterpillars; others went stone picking and one Arthur Brown found work during school hours as a brick-layer; unsurprisingly he failed his 4th Standard but left school shortly afterwards at the age of 13 yrs. to go to sea. What was the point of school if you could earn a much needed copper to help to put food on the table?

For this was the time of the great agricultural depression. It was less than fifty years since the Corn Laws had been repealed heralding free trade and for some time English farming continued as if all was well; there were good harvests and everyone knew that British farming was superior to most of that on the continent. The Crimea followed by the American Civil War protected the grain market from imports from Russia and then America but it was a false security. Prairie farming in America produced cheaper grain, the advent of steam ships meant cheaper transport. Combined with poor harvests in Britain the result was the collapse of British farming. Profits fell; the appearance of the countryside changed with far more pastures and far fewer fields of wheat as farmers made the change from 'corn to horn'. Wages fell and as jobs became scarce many men left the countryside in search of employment, only to find conditions in the industrialised towns to be harsh. For those who remained, such as the families of those children at school in 1890, every penny was hard won and job security fragile, no wonder that the children would go stone-picking or catching caterpillars because the pittance they earned made a difference.

The job of our Schoolmistress must have been both challenging and heartbreaking. Not long after writing her log book, she left the school and became a farmer's wife in a nearby village and in due course the mother of Robert. Born into this farming family in 1909 Bob was to start his schooling at the self-same place of education that his Mother had run some years earlier. And, he too, like so many infants before him had to walk just over 2 miles but he had proper boots and warm clothing.

"The farm was some way from the school, it was quite a walk along the path of the turnpike. Some children had to walk over 3 miles. I can remember the boys would play marbles along the road, and if someone would say, 'Look out there is a car coming' – and that was a very rare occurrence – we would have to get into the side and let the car go past. It was either that or bowling hoops or something. I must have had a slate when I started at 5 yrs. – spit on and rub out. My first memory was of a girl a bit older than me teaching me to knit."

Following his time at the small Church School, the next four years were spent at the Sir John Leman School in Beccles. Looking back it amused him to reflect that he was once in the same year as a potential Nobel Prize winner, "I had the honour of being in the same form as Dorothy Crowfoot (Hodgkin), as one of the boys told me not long back that we generally managed to get ahead of her in the class." He chuckles.

School life may have been taken reasonably seriously, his Mother would have made sure of that, but from his very early years his life was the farm.

"It was a way of life altogether. I mean we didn't want to spend time off the farm, we were a little community of our own; there were 7 or 8 men on the farm. So of course at the weekends and holidays we spent at home on the farm. On Saturdays it was our job, my cousin and myself, to look after the bullocks in the off buildings as the man who looked after them didn't come to work on Saturdays. We had to grind up the pulp and mix up the chaff. Of course we did other jobs with the horses. We had to lead the horse on the horse hoe between the rows; some horses kept their feet nicely between the rows and others were splodging all over everywhere. And harvest, that was a job for us boys, driving the horses with the corn. Then we did lots of rabbiting."

Rabbiting, this was an occupation which started on those boyhood Saturdays and then continued throughout his farming life. Rabbits were an absolute menace decimating the crops and these were the days before myxomatosis and cyanide gassing. Each winter every effort was made to kill as many as possible while they were still marketable. Come early spring the rabbits began to breed as only rabbits do. As Bob so prosaically put it, "Not unlike the old Patriarchs of the Old Testament where Abraham begat Isaac and Isaac begat Jacob etc., only with these promisucous animals it was 2 begat 4 which begat 8 which begat 16 which begat 32, and so on all season." Keeping the numbers down was a major job.

He continues, "Killing off all these rabbits was a lot of work for the gamekeepers and found work at certain times for full time warreners as well. Various methods were used, such as trapping, snaring, ferreting, netting and shooting. Apart from the professionals lots of people got a lot of sport from rabbiting and they started young in those days. A quite common sight on a Saturday would be two or three boys with a terrier dog and a spade walking round the fields. The dog would scent a rabbit in a hole and if this was heavy land area the holes would not be very long or deep, often no more than 'bolt holes'. Out of someone's pocket would come a 'shut-knife' and a long bramble or briar or bramble cut from the hedge and the thorns trimmed off the bottom for handling. This was pushed into the hole, twisted round a bit, withdrawn and examined for rabbit's fur. If there was anyone at home a little digging to bring the occupant within arm's reach and hey presto, like the conjuror's hat out would come a rabbit.

"It was a good sport during the winter months to go out with a long net at night time, the darker the better with a bit of breeze and if there was some rain in the offing so much the better as the rabbits seemed to know and would come out to feed before it started. The art was to get between them and their home as quickly and quietly as possible, so you wanted the wind in the right direction so they couldn't hear you. The net or nets usually 50 or 100 yards long were run out and held up about 2ft high by sticks, about every 10 or 12 yards. They ran on two cords or 'reins', one at top and one at the bottom which were pulled tight and pegged down at each end. The next thing was to get behind the rabbits which meant a wide detour and this is where a well trained dog came in handy as he would chase them into the net and then go back for more. An untrained dog would just go wild, kill them in the net, spoiling the rabbits and tearing the net. If working with a mate, one would stay with the net and by keeping hold of the top rein would feel when a rabbit hit it. He would then locate it and get it out quickly before it had time to squeal and warn the others and before it got tangled up too much. This they certainly did sometimes as the size of the mesh was such that the rabbit just got its head through. There was plenty of slack as the nets were made with about 150 yards of net to 100 yards of rein. This meant that after a few frantic efforts to get free there was quite an entanglement of net and rabbit which took a bit of sorting out, in addition to which if in too long the captive would try to bite its way out which wasn't too good for the net.

"One night my Father, who knew nothing of netting rabbits, thought he would like to come with me to see what went on. Jays Hill, now a young forest of trees, was then a mass of gorse bushes, bracken, brambles and rabbit warrens, and this we had to cross. It was pitch dark but I knew my way by instinct and a few dim landmarks. I suppose I went a bit too fast at first as poor Dad was soon lost, so as soon as I found him again he hung onto my coat tails for the rest of the way. I got everything set up ready and left him with instructions what to do if he felt a tug on the rein, and made my detour with Nipper, my black and tan terrier, to the low meadows where the rabbits would be out feeding – or so we hoped. I hadn't been gone long when a signal came through to the end that the net had made a capture, so off went Father to investigate. He soon located it and through the darkness could discern a wriggling mass which he promptly pounced on. But oh what a calamity! The capture was not a rabbit but a hedgehog! Perhaps it was just as well that I was not on hand to hear what I imagine was a rather one-sided conversation and I don't think an eavesdropper would have gathered from what the poor animal was called that it wasn't either a rabbit or a hedgehog but could have been quite sure that it was of doubtful parentage. Eventually we finished with ten rabbits and after disentangling our prickly friend we packed up and made for home. I was glad of some help as half a score of rabbits, nets and stick would have been quite a load had I been alone. And so to bed, and I can assure anyone that after an expedition like that there is no need to count sheep or rabbits to get to sleep; it just came naturally. The fresh night air and strenuous exercise was better than any sleeping pills."

Before leaving the topic of rabbiting, Bob, always with a sense of humour, was keen to share a joke with a little rabbit story from West Suffolk – "The Breckland area around Brandon was notorious for its rabbit population. In fact it was big business and they were caught and sent to London literally by the truckload. There was a butcher in Brandon who had quite a reputation for his rabbit pies and pasties which he used to bake and sell in his shop. One day a visitor, who had found them very much to his liking, quizzed the old man to try to find out what the secret was. 'Oh', he said, 'there's no secret abut them, just a bit of rabbit and a bit of hoss-meat.' This rather startled the enquirer but as the old boy seemed quite serious he said, 'Oh yes, but what proportion would it be?' to which he got the reply, 'Just half and half. One rabbit to one hoss.'"

Country boys like Bob and his friends were never idle; as well as rabbiting, boys were expected to go bird-nesting. There were no restrictions on such a hobby in those days. Water hens' eggs were to eat of course but the other eggs were just for a collection. The fact that people can no longer plunder nests has got to be a good thing but the children then were respectful of the birds, taking only one egg for a nest and along the way learning a great deal about the birds and their habits.

"Of course we all had guns at that time, an air gun or something. Sparrows were quite a menace in the cornstacks, and it would be nothing to put some chaff down, hide up in the barn with a 12 bore gun, shoot into them and kill ten or twelve at a time. There was a constant war on sparrows; you could catch them at night time or evening out at the stacks.

They would get in the stacks for shelter and you would have what was called a chaff sieve, and you would put it on a fork so that you could hold it, and you would put it on the stack, you would hear something flutter and you would catch a sparrow, wring his neck and he was gone. They used to pay, the District Council, a farthing a head for sparrows and a penny a tail for rats, rats' tails. Rats again, that was a regular job, we had good fun ferreting for rats."

Like rabbiting, dealing with rats was a job once learnt in boyhood that stood him in good stead on the farm in later life. – "I used to go round every night winter times with a torch and a 410 gun and shoot the rats because they were all over everywhere. A favourite place you would see them running up the chains that were hanging where the mangers were, that would be a favourite spot and you would shoot them going up there. I nearly always had a good ratter, a little terrier dog, and she would watch me at night time when I was sitting down and I would only have to say 'Rats' and she would be ready to go out. They didn't want training, that came naturally. I nearly killed one of them once. There was a hurdle up and a rat had gone into that and she was at one end and I was at the other waiting for the rat to come out and something moved you see and I'd got my stick like this and I came down right like that; of course that was her. I thought I had killed her, I'd knocked her unconscious, but she was alright… well, after a bit. I had gun dogs but I never had one that was any good really because they were all spoilt. If I had a dog that would catch a rabbit she wouldn't bring it to me," he laughs. "They always followed me around, if anyone came onto the farm they would say, 'Where's Bob?' and the reply would be, 'I don't know but the dog is there so he isn't far off'."

Before we leave Bob's childhood, and we have already wandered a little as from being a youth on the farm it was what appeared to be a seamless progression into adult farm work, however, whilst a boy he had a pet lamb…"We separated all the milk for making butter and the children used to come all that way up the road, about ½ mile, with cans and they could have skimmed milk, 4 pints for a penny. I saw an old boy at Mutford once and he said, 'I remember coming up to your farm for milk and your Mother would say, '4 pints for a penny' and I would give her the penny and she would say, 'Now you sing me a song and you can have your penny back' and we did.' At that time I had a pet lamb and as it grew up the children who come up for milk, they used to tease it a bit, sort of push it. Then it began to get rather big and masterful and one day we heard some screams and there were two or three children in the horse pond, the lamb was on the brink and they were in there with their cans and daren't come out. He had chased them. We made a cart to put him in, we put the wheels on, made some shafts and a collar to fit and got Sooty in, started him off, away he went but he didn't get round the corner, the cart caught on the corner and of course he was free. At that time the cow shed there had half doors and he used to get in and get the cows' food and that used to annoy our milkman and if he saw Sooty there you would hear a scuffle and you would see Sooty come right over the top. Then we bought two more to go with him so there were three, and I was going to be away for the weekend and the boy from the next farm was going to come and feed my lambs for me and he tried to keep Sooty away from the other two so they could get some food but Sooty just knocked him over. When he was being brought up he was an orphan lamb at the neighbouring farm and my cousin, that was Dot, she used to feed him with the bottle and she went away for the weekend or something and that lamb would not touch a thing from anyone else, not till she come back, so he was 2 or 3 days without food."

The lamb was only one of a series of pets that Bob had throughout his childhood and into his married life. Olive, who became his wife, takes up the story of two other animals who became part of their lives. "We had two pigs and they were tame; they used to come to the door and come for a walk. One of them in particular used to follow us up the lane. One of my aunts came, very prim and proper and always so clean and lovely, and we went for a walk up the hill and there was this manure heap at the top and it had been raining and there was water all around, pigs love all that, this one went and rolled in that and shook herself all over Aunt Nellie." One wonders if Aunt Nellie came to stay again.

"There was a horse sale just once a year in Beccles, the other was the weekly market for bullocks. May was Bungay May Fair and that was the day they used to turn the cattle out onto the marshes. They wouldn't turn the horses out to grass before Bungay May Fair, it didn't matter whether it was rain, snow or blow they would have to go out then but never before then. Now they turn them out about April, before the weather has turned warmer. In those days there were very few sheep in our district, and not many cows either, mainly fattening bullocks and just a few cows for butter-making; then it gradually got on that they changed over to dairy and they sent it away; churns would be taken to Beccles station for transportation."

Bob helped with most things. "Yes, I've made butter from beginning to end. My Mother was ill for a while so I did the churning, that was usually the wife's job, I got quite expert. Churned it first, sometimes it would come quickly, sometimes not, then you strained that off and that went into a big long trough affair with rollers on and that worked to get the butter milk out of it and it was solid and knocked up into a block; and you had to weigh it up into pounds and half pounds. I only did it a few times but I got so that I really didn't need the scales, I would know just by judgement how much to put on, and then knock them up into shape. I expect you have seen them round ones with the press on the top."

There was a buzz and vibrancy on market day in the nearby town when from all around the country folk poured into the town to shop or bringing their own produce to sell. Farmers came to the Corn Exchange and gathered for a mardle in the street outside, whilst their wives brought their eggs, butter and any other seasonal goods to sell, and, of course, it was a chance to meet friends and have a good gossip. The streets rang out to the sound of pony and traps and carriers' wagons as they converged from all directions, putting up at the various public houses. Coming in from the Shadingfield Road, Bob's Mother, going into Beccles on a Friday would leave her pony and trap at the Cross Keys; others, from Barsham and Shipmeadow way used the Angel and from Ellough and the Lowestoft Road the Black Boy; coming in from Norfolk over the bridge it may have been the Horse and Groom. During the first war Bob's Mother had regular customers for her butter and eggs and should she have any left over she would take them to the Co-op where the manager was grateful for these extra supplies and consequently this friendship meant that the family rarely went short of groceries.

So it was that when he left school at 16 years old Bob automatically followed in the footsteps of his Grandfather and Father; he was the only son. Perhaps if there had been two or three boys it may have been different. However as Bob explains, the farming he knew in his early life was a challenging occupation.

"During the 20's and 30's farming got very difficult, it was a bad time, but then when Hitler was on the rise that revived and things bucked up a bit. Farm labourers didn't earn much then, 28 shillings a week for a labourer, not a lot. They lived in farm cottages but you couldn't charge them more than 3 shillings a week for rent. In the 1920s the price of corn was very low but you just had to take it as it came. I can remember at the low time we had a sample of barley which was sold to the mill for

16 shillings a coomb, which was 2cwts, and they couldn't move it because they couldn't sell it again and eventually they sold it for 12 shillings a coomb for grinding, so they had to lose. You would come into Beccles corn market every Friday with your samples, there were no contracts in those days. In the corn market there were little stands and the local grain merchants and agricultural machinery people; anyone who was doing business would have a stand there every Friday. You would take your samples of corn along to sell, there were no testings then, it was all done by looking at it, rubbing your hand; but there was no going back, it was all done on faith and word of mouth, you did your deal and you would stand up to it, no gazumping or anything. A deal was a deal. Cattle market was by auction. Up on Norwich Hill they sold privately, it was all done like that (he slaps his hands) and that was that."

To make things worse in the 1920s there was an epidemic of Foot & Mouth disease, which swept across the continent, the virus carried from country to country by various means. Then, just as things had begun to pick up during and following the war there was another epidemic throughout Europe. The British method of dealing with the virus was diametrically opposed to that on the continent in those days; we pursued a slaughtering policy with the State paying compensation; in Europe they favoured vaccination. In 1923 there were nearly two thousand outbreaks: 69,000 cattle were lost, 26,000 sheep and 33,000 pigs. To face the problem again in the 1950s must have been devastating...

"It was about 1952, near the time of the big storm when so many trees blew down because we had a big evergreen oak in the front and there were three arms on it and one of them blew right over into the house. They had had Foot & Mouth at the neighbouring farm the year before; I got involved with that because I was the one that diagnosed it. I used to take the milk into Lowestoft and it was a Sunday morning and I used to get the Sunday papers and drop them in as I came back. When I got there the girl Ruth says, 'Can you help me milk a cow that I can't milk?' so we had to tie the legs up and what not and we milk the cow and then she said, 'Father says (he was in bed) would you look at the young things, he doesn't like the look of them.' So I looked over and there was one of them that was making a smacking noise with its mouth, so I rang up the vet and went on home. The next day the policeman came and said , 'I hear you've been on the next farm, we've got to take your clothes to be fumigated.' My biggest concern was that I had a little watch pocket and I always kept a ten shilling note in there, quite a lot of money in those days and the breeches went away and everything and they came back fumigated and it was still there."

It was the following year that Bob had to deal with the problem on his own farm as the epidemic struck. "Our two pigs were killed, they gave me a lot of money for them, £20 I think. At that time they were saving the carcases for human consumption; they just cut the heads off. There was a gang of butchers down at the slaughterers, they took all the cows and the biggest of the stock, that was about all they had time for. Then the smaller ones they didn't have time for they just dug a big trench and buried them. The pigs they just cut the heads off ; took all the carcases away so we had a great tumbril full of pigs' heads and guts. And the cats, we had to keep them shut up so they didn't carry it to someone else. I had taken out an insurance just two weeks before we got Foot & Mouth. The vet who came who was in charge, he was a Welshman, he didn't know much about country life and pheasants he was quite interested in. So I said, 'We'll have a walk round with a gun,' course a rented farm we didn't have the shooting rights see; 'Don't bother,' he said, 'If the keepers come I'll soon get rid of them, they mustn't come onto your farm.' He'd never had a pheasant so we gave him one to send back to Wales."

The Oxford dictionary defines 'to farm' as to cultivate land. It sounds so simple; farming is growing crops and rearing livestock for food for the nation. The purpose of the industry has not changed for generations but do those young men in the massive machines which now dominate our countryside, machines with all the latest computer technology, feel any link to those farmers to whom the advent of the first tractors and then combiners felt a bewildering change, men, like Bob, some of whose warmest memories were working with horses on the land?

"I first ploughed with a horse when I left school, it was all horses then until the Second World War. There were eight horses and two horsemen on the farm. We never had tractors at that time. Both men and horses were wise in their ways and like people in other walks of life there were always some outstanding characters who impressed themselves on your memory and it only needs a little nostalgic thinking to bring them back into full focus.

"I remember one old horse in particular, Captain by name, I'm not saying that he could tell the time but he always knew when it was leaving-off time. Our farm was a bit one-ended as lots of farms tend to be – house and buildings having to be near the road I suppose, and because of this our horsemen worked their horses what was called 'one journey'. This meant they did not come back to the farm at mid-day but worked through with a short dinner break in the field until 3 o'clock, by which time the horses were ready for a meal and getting rather sluggish. Captain in particular – a bit of an 'old soldier' – needed a little jogging to keep going. These fields were within earshot of the London to Beccles railway – L.N.E.R. in those days, or was it the Great Eastern? There was always a train due to pass along at that time. I'm not sure if it was blowing its whistle coming down or puffing its way up, but in any case clearly audible often to Captain before anyone else and his pace immediately quickened and his counterpart in the furrow (Captain being the 'land' horse) was kept nearly half a length behind despite all efforts to keep up. If they were going away from the leaving-off end of the field when he heard the train it was a quick turn round at the end and care had to be taken that it wasn't too quick with a foot over the trace and complications that followed.

"Ours was an eight-horse farm and the names that come to my mind with Captain were Smart, Gyp, Tinker, Boxer, Depper, Kitty and Bowler. They all had their different characteristics which often determined which job they were put to. Those that walked wide when ploughing had to be 'land' horses and walk on the unploughed land; those that walked more daintily, putting one foot in front of the other, were 'furrow' horses; that is they walked in the furrow. These latter were chosen when the time came round for horse-hoeing, to walk between the rows of the root crops, as they were not so likely to stand on the small plants in their early stages, or later when they got larger to kick them up.

"At harvest and haysel some were better as thill horses – in the shafts – others in front as trace horses; the same thing

AND I LOOKED BACK

applying when carting in the roots or carting out the muck. Tinker, although strong and steady could not be used in the shafts, as being slightly 'jinked' or weak in the back could not back a cart, so was always a trace horse. I remember seeing the horse dealers or prospective buyers at horse sales or farm auctions looking in the horses' mouths to see by their teeth how old they were and then making them walk backwards to see if they were 'jinked'.

"If any of the horses were vicious and given to kicking the others when on the meadow or in the horse-yard they would have to wear a 'clog' – a piece of wood fixed by a short chain and strapped to one of their hind feet.

"It took years of experience for the true horseman to build up that relationship and knowledge of the horses he worked with; but one piece of useful information that was passed down was about telling a horse's age by its teeth.

> To tell the age of any horse
> Inspect the lower jaw of course.
>
> 2 middle nippers you behold
> Before the colt is two weeks old;
> Before 8 weeks 2 more will come;
> Before 8 months the "corners" cut the gum.
>
> The outside grooves will disappear
> From middle 2 in just one year;
> In 2 years from the 2nd pair;
> In 3 the corners too are bare.
>
> At 2 the middle nippers drop,
> At 3 the second pair can't stop;
> When 4 years old the 3rd pair goes
> At 5 a full new set he shows.

The deep black spots wil pass from view
At 6 years from the middle 2;
The 2nd pair at 7 years;
At 8 the spot each corner clears;

From middle nippers, upper jaw
At 9 the black spots will withdraw;
The 2nd pair at 10 are white,
11 finds the corners white.

As time goes on, as horsemen know,
The oval teeth 3-sided grow;
They longer get, project before
Till 20, when we know no more."

Despite the bond between man and horse and many who believed that the weight of heavy machinery did far more damage to the land than horses ever could, change was progress which was inevitable. "Changes have been so gradual that you don't notice it. Biggest change must have been from horses to machinery I suppose. Our first tractor was during the war but we still kept horses at the same time. Tractors would only do part of the work. I mean, you had to gradually adapt. When they came in originally you would do just your main cultivation, ploughing; then later on you had to adapt your self binder and clipper to make them to be able to be drawn by a tractor see. We had some sort of device, not one of Jack's vapourisers [see 'Jack'] because originally the tractors started on petrol and then turned over to T.V.O., so you had got to get them warmed up."

At the same time as Bob was getting used to his first tractor his future wife, Olive, then serving in the Royal Air Force, was enjoying her first experience of driving tractors, little thinking it would stand her in good stead later in life on the farm. This time, though, she was delivering the bombs to three different aircraft. Agreeing with Bob, she remembered those early tractors as having 'personality'; with no self-starters it had been quite a challenge to get them going.

"I can't really remember when we hadn't got a self binder, before that it was all mowing, mowing everything you see, even the barley which had clover in it. With a scythe, there would be 6 or 7 of the men anyhow, one behind the other just mowing like that [he demonstrates the movement]. I did one year when I was quite a boy, I couldn't do the full width then, I had to do a half one. It was quite a skill and if you could sharpen your scythe you could mow all right but if you couldn't sharpen the scythe it was twice the work."

Olive tried to use a fiddle for sowing the clover seed. The fiddle was a wooden box which she described as being vaguely in the shape of a violin; some had handles, big heavy things which were spun round thus dispersing the clover and grass seed. However, she left the fiddle to the men and preferred to sow the seed by hand. As with any other farmer's wife Olive kept the chickens, but as ever it was in the farm kitchen that she ruled. "All you read about these days is dumplings! Bob used to like barley swimmers but I never see the sense of making those because it is only flour and water; put some suet in them and there is more goodness. I suppose they made them originally in the working class as cheaply as they could, just flour and water and they had got a dumpling. We never made boiled batter pudding but when I first came across that I had taken an aunt to a relation of hers on a farm and we were staying to dinner and up comes – I don't know if it was batter pudding now or dumplings with gravy, so I thought to myself, 'This is a funny sort of dinner', so ate that. Then the next thing that comes in is a great big sirloin of beef, and, of course, they were hacking that off in great pieces."

Bob had obviously always been well looked after as he looks back fondly to the kitchen of his boyhood. "I've been lucky all my life with cooks! I remember early, when I was quite young, I can remember them making rusks and bread in a brick oven, and that was fed with faggots. Deep as that with just an opening in the front to get these faggots in and they actually tied them up specially for baking day when they were hedge cutting. That was Thursdays and this brick oven would be heated with those, there was no grating or anything and once it was hot and they were burnt out they would rake the ashes out and then it was ready to put the bread or whatever it was, they had to put a long pole called a peeler with a spade on the end to go under the things and push them in till they were done. The last thing of all was putting in the rusks, which they split, you must never cut them but break them, and they would go back to be browned off. Meat would be cooked on the range, or the little Dutch oven which we had built into the wall."

Olive smiles. "I was lucky, I just escaped that, I had a Raeburn."

"In the old scullery place at Moat Farm there was a brick oven, open fire with the hobs each side, three coppers of three different sizes, two pumps. One pump was soft water and one was hard, each side of the big stone sink. We saved the water from the roof, separate well, and then the other was a well for drinking water. One lorry driver who had a drink thought it was so lovely he took it back to Newcastle or somewhere, he'd never tasted water like that before.

"We didn't brew beer but I can remember others brewing for haysel and for harvest, about twice for threshing times and once with double strength for Christmas. They filled about three big nine gallon casks. When we had a lot of apples we took them and and got them pressed at St. Andrew's or we went to a place at Westhall where the horse used to go round and round and they used to make the cider. They had all these apples in this moat sort of thing and the horse would walk round and round and grind them all up and get all the liquid juice. They had a press as well but they had to grind them first because they had to be small to go into the presses where there were layers of canvas or something and they didn't take whole apples, they took the mulch. Once it had been mulched up a chap down in the village used to make our cider, I used to take him the sugar too. Then he rigged up a press of his own, you've been used to seeing one that screwed down, well he had a much better idea than that, he just put a hydraulic jack on the top – much easier. My first introduction to cider, I think, was Mr Kent's, he used to make quite a bit and he was helping us when we were converting the cottages. He said one day, 'Will you be my executor?'

I said, "Yes, one condition, when you have gone I want one of those barrels of cider; not that I want you to go in a hurry." I knew he kept them a long while and they were strong. He did die a year or two later, and nearly the first thing his daughter said was, 'Your barrel of cider is there.' So we had that bottled up and that really was strong stuff."

Olive remembered folk in the country making a lot of wine. "I used to go Red Cross collecting and one of the people was collecting dandelions to make wine, and cowslips and your Mother used to make parsnip wine, it was just like champagne and very intoxicating. Then, of course, we made jams – damson, bullace and strawberry. I was good at strawberry. Plums were good for bottling using Kilner jars. We had a canning machine mainly for the strawberries; it was very professional, you did twenty turns and it was folding the lid over; twenty turns of the handle and you had done it properly, then you used to have to put it into boiling water for two or three minutes. They would last for ages. You used to have to send to London for the tins but then they became too expensive."

This was the time before fridges, when many people grew their own vegetables and in the country many had their own pig. "We salted runner beans and meat had to be cured, we took it down to Beccles as it had to be smoked. Then, with the ham I used to get a bag of malt cones and put them in the middle of that and hang them up in the barn till we wanted them and that would absorb anything if there was any superage from the joint. All the hooks were in the ceiling down at the farm. Bob's father used to make bloaters out of herrings. He had this iron cylinder and brass stair rods and you used to thread these fish through the gills and hang them over the top of this chimney. It was just a tub, with the top and bottom out, on a few bricks. He'd get a little fire going with oak shavings, put these herrings across the top and there you had got a smoke house. I remember letting the air in and it flared once. You see at that time there was a food shortage but there was always a glut of herring, they weren't so much each, you could get a bag of them for a shilling [5p] I suppose, and, of course, we had connections at Lowestoft, so they would come back with a bag full of herring. They were nice weren't they?"

Herrings were the cheap yet nourishing food during times when the greater part of the population was not in any way affluent and when many in the rural communties were struggling to make ends meet. Perhaps things during Bob's farming days were not as dire as those years remembered in his Mother's school log book but hard times make people provident and Bob and Olive were always resourceful. He remembers the days when threshing was done with a steam engine and it was really dirty work. "Everything used to get bunged up. The amount of dust and stuff that was coming to the tractor and the fans, you see, would actually draw it into the radiator instead of drawing air in and you had to keep it clear." So Bob invented and patented Robol to help solve the problem. "It really was only of use to thrashing people and there weren't enough of those. If it had been something that went on an ordinary farm tractor there would have been a good demand; I suppose we sold one to every county in the country but not enough to do much good."

"It was just fun while it lasted," said Olive

Those last words of Olive summed up their attitude to life. They worked hard, very hard, and they enjoyed every aspect of it. They produced much of their own food whether it be in the field, the hedgerow, dairy or kitchen and their hospitality was unstinting. Their farming 'family' was important to them but so too was the wider community as Bob showed by his interest in local government. Never idle, he enjoyed working with wood and in retirement he continued to make his own very individual walking sticks, making the handles with holly and using whatever other kinds of wood which came his way for the rest of the sticks. As he approached his 90th birthday and not in the best of health, he taught himself to do decoupage.

His lasting legacy was the parish magazine which he launched as a way of helping a rather isolated community to share its news. That magazine now has outstripped what would have been his wildest dreams and serves not just one or two villages, but fifteen. It is valued now more than ever. Part of his contribution to the magazine in those early days was his creation of 'Ephraim' who first featured in this magazine and then moved on to be appreciated by a wider readership in a local paper. Bob's purpose in inventing Ephraim was to raise a smile or two, so let us give Ephraim the final words...

"Ephraim was enjoying a tankard of cider under his apple tree while his missus was busy pushing a barrow load of manure up the garden path.

Willum popped his head over the fence and told Ephraim he didn't think his missus should be pushing a heavy load like that.

'No, bor, I know,' said Ephraim 'I've told her time and agin she oughter be pullin' on ut!'"

2
HARRY
ESCAPE TO SEA

It was a new century and just along the coast from Lowestoft, Great Yarmouth was gaining the reputation as the herring capital of the world. Crans of herring lined the quayside waiting to be carried off to be salted, pickled or smoked before being quickly despatched to countries round the world, meeting the vast demand from Germany and Poland, Russia and America. Fishing with its many associated trades, whether they were treating the fish, making the famous bloater paste, making nets and building and repairing ships, combined with tourism in boosting the town's economy. Serving both industries were the three stations in the town; as with Lowestoft, the railway brought wealth. Mainly working-class tourists spilt out of the trains coming from the Midlands and the South. They would find an aquarium, the Winter Gardens and in 1908 the first purpose-built picture house in the country. Everything was buoyant and then in 1914 came war and the town's income plummeted.

When Harry was born in 1921 in the aftermath of the First World War the town was trying desperately hard to rebuild its failing economy. There was a road-widening scheme and a new swimming pool, race course and boating lakes. Then came the return of the Scottish fisher girls who packed their kist with all their basic needs – bedding, clothing, gutting knives and, of course, their knitting needles and wool. The herring were back. Fishing had been resumed and the catches were starting to recover. Harry was the eldest of six, the son of a fisherman who worked on the drifters going out of Great Yarmouth. Despite the herring fishermen being amongst the most prosperous of the East Anglian fishing community life was hard, not least on the women like Harry's mother. As soon as the children were old enough they would all earn a few pence in the early mornings before school by going bird scaring on the nearby fruit farm. Scraping together every penny to keep a family of six children in the 1930s meant that young Harry's contribution was a boon.

Harry recalls, "He kept us all employed, all the while. I was the eldest so, of course, if anything happened it was my fault because I should have seen that it didn't happen."

Was this his employer holding him to account or his father, with whom he certainly had an abrasive relationship as being away at sea much of the time he seemed to feel that his eldest son didn't live up to his expectations.

Without any regret Harry left school as soon as he possibly could at the age of fourteeen and he didn't have to look far for work.

"My first full-time job was on the strawberry farm. There were acres and acres; half was strawberries and the other half a poultry farm. The owner was an architect and he used to keep us occupied during the winter months by building a cottage or bungalow or something on part of the land near the road. The old boy used to say to me, 'If you like come early in the morning I'll leave the gun, it was a 410, and cartridges in there and you can do a bit of scaring.' So I used to get paid overtime, that weren't much for about an hour. I used to get up about 4 o'clock, bike down the back lane, get the gun out of the packing shed, cock it full of cartridges, then at the back of the house there was a big meadow and it was alive with rabbits and I thought to myself, 'Well, I don't know there's a lot of dinners running about there,' so one or two mornings I sort of went round and knocked over a rabbit.

"The old boy said to me one morning, 'There's a lot of birds at the back of the house ain't there Harry?'

I say, 'Yeh, there are some long ears an' all.'

He say, 'Yes, I could do with a couple of them one of these mornings.'

I said, 'Alright, I'll get you a couple in the morning.'

"He used to lay there in bed in the mornings and he knew the sound of where the shots come from, behind the house not up in the strawberry fields. That worked alright, he used to tell me when he wanted a couple, I used to go round and knock m'self off a couple at the same time. Mother was pleased. My first wage on the farm was 6s 3d [31p], it was 7 shillings and he stopped 9 pence for a stamp. Then the first summer, because I had been there as a youngster and knew how to carry on and how to pick, he say to me, 'Harry, I am going to put your money up."

I said, 'Oh yeh, what have I got to do for that.?'

He grinned at me, 'I want you, you're part of the staff, you might as well be on the same footing as them. 30s a week [£1.50], a full man's money.'

He used to say, 'Go on Harry, get your bike, go down to Norton's.'

"This was by the tramway at Gorleston. I used to go down there and get him a box of 500 Players No. 3, they're the oval ones, not round. That was my Friday afternoon trip; I used to bike down to Gorleston and get his cigarettes, they used to last him a week."

The 1931 census showed unemployment in Gt. Yarmouth was as high as 20%. Famous for its Rows – narrow lanes leading off the Quay with tiny houses, these were home to many of the poorest. Whilst Harry was potting the odd rabbit for his family's table, a journalist from the Yarmouth Mercury was visiting the Rows and reporting on the conditions to be found. Homes with damp walls and rotting floorboards, where rats and cockroaches were the norm swarming into food cupboards; boots and clothing had to be shaken out in the morning. One home had rain coming through the roof and the children all slept together in one room because of the size of the rats in another one. Life wasn't easy for Harry and his family but it was not as bad as it was for many living in those crowded, dark unhealthy places.

"I got fed up as Dad and I had one of our usual set-tos one Friday and I said to him, 'I'm getting fed up with this, I'll clear off to sea.'

'Huh,' he said, 'you, you're too scared to leave your mother's apron strings.'

'Oh yeh.' I never said no more and I took a day off and went down to Lowestoft where I knew a Skipper who was getting ready to go to Scotland, the Shetlands, for the summer. So, I went to see him. There was me and another young chap from Belton who wanted to get away an' all.

'What you want to get away for?'

'Well, Dad and I can't agree, when I want to go playing football he want me on the garden and one thing and another, so I've decided I'm clearing off.'

'Do he know?'

'No, and don't you tell him neither. I'll tell him.'

He signed us both on. He said to me, 'You can have the cook's job if you like.'

'If that's all you are going to offer me I don't want it.'

'Well,' he say, 'you can have the cast-off's job; if you're half as good as the old man you'll be alright.'

"That's how I started. A boy named Billy Grimmer from

Belton, he took the cook's job and I was to be a deck hand. That was on the Friday, I worked Saturday on the fruit farm when I gave my notice in.'"

For the time being that was to be the end of his work on the land; back on the farm his employer was obviously sorry to lose him.

"He say to me, 'Going to sea isn't all fun.'

'I know, 'cause I've been with Dad on a couple of trips.'

He say, 'It's alright when it's fine, but when they go up and down…'

I say, 'Well that's a chance I've got to take.'

"On the Monday we started what they call rigging out, getting the ship ready to go to Scotland, getting nets and ropes aboard and all the stores and what have you. I used to leave home bike through to Lowestoft, from Bradwell I used to bike through to Blundeston and that way to Lowestoft, about 8 mile that was. Then work there during the day, bike home again and get there about the same time I would have done from the strawberry farm.

"Thursday night the Skipper say, 'You won't want to go in tomorrow, be at Lowestoft 8 o'clock Monday morning with your gear ready to sail.'

I said, 'Alright.' and went home and said to Dad, 'You won't want to call me in the morning I ain't going to work'

'You ain't what!!!!'

'No, day off.'

'Why?'

'Well, I finished. I don't work on the farm any more. I'm going to sea on Monday morning. I'm going to Scotland.'

He wouldn't believe it and he went indoors to Mother. 'That boy reckons he's going fishing.'

'Yes, didn't you know? He's been working at Lowestoft all week getting ready.'

'What's he doing for gear?'

When I went in he says, 'Mother tells me you are going to sea on Monday. What made your mind up to that?'

I said, 'You did.'

He never said no more for a bit.

Then, 'How are you going to get your gear?'

'You can get it at Yarmouth Stores and pay on the trip.' Yarmouth Stores at Gorleston would supply you with your gear providing you left so much a week from your pay.

'No boy of mine is starting work in debt. We'll go down to Yarmouth Stores in the morning and we'll get everything you want.'

"And he rigged me out from seaboots to oilskin apron, oilskin frock, souwester, all the rest of it, couple of thick woollen pullovers. He rigged me completely out and he said, 'There you are, it's up to you now. You want to go to sea and don't say I drove you to it.'

'Well you hev.'"

Home for the next three months was now on a steam drifter. "That was the only steam boat I was on, a drifter called The Norfolk Sutling; that was the name of the fishing firm at Lowestoft. LT685, I can still remember the number!" Harry points to an oil painting of his ship and another of The Ocean Swell. "That was the one my Dad was on, it went out of Yarmouth. We used to go up to Shetland every summer, we had good Scotch fishing. Everytime we went out of harbour I was sick for two or three hours and then for the rest of the trip I was alright. Later when I was in the Merchant Navy it used to be the same, the first couple of hours I used to be bad then after that the ship could roll itself over and it didn't worry me. I was a deckhand on the drifter. I was up in the bows when they were shooting nets; you have the main sinker rope running out and every so often they'd fasten a net corner to this rope you see, and there were buoys, you know, the floats that held the nets up in the water and that was my job to fasten these buoys on, one at a time as the net cord, the net rope, as that was going out every twelve foot two half hitches, that was all. It was quite easy when you got the hang of it. Then when we hauled we used to go into the rope room and coil the rope, round and round and round. Hauled in with a steam winch. You passed the net rope, the big thick rope which the nets were fastened to, and you would take two or three turns round the capstan and pull them in. My job then was up in the bows and as the net rope come in I would untie 'em and hook them inside and then when they went down the net rope would just lift them off and let them go as they took the nets down. We used to shoot twice a day, nets out for about twelve hours, an early morning one and then a late one which would be all night. You would just hang there at the end of the rope, at night you would see all the other boats' anchor lights, well not anchor lights, they had a lamp which they used to put up when they'd got the nets out and it was like being in a little town with all these lights all the way round. We just drifted, the engines were shut down, there was an engineer on duty in case of an emergency or anything like that, because now and agin you'd get some of these coasters, they used to sail right across and cut your nets – nobody must get in their way! They are bigger than you so... When we were drifting because we were not needed in the engine room we were on watch. We had to take a watch with the rest of them just in case; sometimes the wind would turn and blow you across the nets or something like that, we had to steam out then and get them in the right direction – so you were always on call.

"When we came home my Dad and I made up. I had quite a bit of money to draw 'cause we only used to draw sort of pocket money all the while we were away. I left money at home for my Mother, you know, to help her out. I had what I wanted and the old Skipper when we went into a sale ground he would always sell a couple of cran on the side. That was called 'stocky' and he used to share that out amongst us crew for pocket money. Yes we had a good Skipper and Mate. Every time we went in there was a cran or a couple of cran of herrin' that went to the stocky fund. As a 16 year old I think I got about 24 shillings [£1.20] a week. Mind you, you got your food and everything else. Mother banked my money although I left it for her but she said, 'You aren't here, you're not costing us nothing,' so she banked it in my name. That's how I got started, it was more money than I would have got on land.

"So, I had a few pounds when I got home and I bought myself a new bike. It was 7 guineas. Well, my Dad, he created, 'You can get a Hercules for £3 10s! You'll learn.'"

No wonder his Father was so appalled. It was the 1930's, the country was in the grip of depression with mass unemployment. Industrial wages had fallen to about 1s 6d [7p] an hour, agricultural wages were no more than when Harry left the farm, just around £1 10s for a fifty hour week.

The advent of bicycles had provided cheap transport for the masses. The army, who had used the Cycle Brigade back in the 1880's, introduced them into their regiments on a bigger scale in the 1914 war. These Cycle Corps were invaluable for reconnaissance and communication work with the added advantage that cyclists did not suffer from sore feet and a bicycle did not have to be fed and cared for as did the horse. These cycle battalions were disbanded in th early 1920s but at home it became the most common form of transport, particularly for the working man. Even Harry as a young teenager in a poor family had an old bike but now with an unexpected windfall in the shape of the bank balance his Mother had built up for him he really could not resist buying something special. Seven whole guineas! Of course his Father thought he was extravagant and he had a point

This top of the range bicycle, with a hard seat and probably high handlebars – and did it even have gears? – opened up Harry's horizons and it was now time to look further afield for better paid work; so he headed inland on what was going to be a fateful expedition. First, from his home village of Bradwell just outside Great Yarmouth he headed for Norwich where he stopped for some refreshment and then on towards Beccles, a market town on the River Waveney which formed the county boundary between Norfolk and Suffolk. Various coasters travelled up the Waveney and this is where he thought he might find a position. Cycling over the marshes Harry then stopped on the bridge by the The Ship Inn watching the youngsters on a sandy site below, which he later learnt they called the Flat, where you could walk under the bridge. He got talking to one of the young fellows who invited him to meet his father, an old army regimental sergeant major. Not surprisingly Harry was a little apprehensive. 'I don't know I want to meet him!' However he braved it, they made him a cup of tea and introduced him to Violet, one of the five children. Vi' as she was always known was to become his wife for over fifty years.

Occasional wherries and a number of coasters were still to be seen on the rivers of East Anglia in the mid 30s but their time was gradually coming to an end as the faster and more efficient rail and road traffic took over. There was nothing quite like the sight of the wherries. They could have been called the Viking ships of the 19th and 20th centuries, pointed at bow and stern, wooden hull and those glorious brown sails which blended so well with the landscape of broad and river. Their great hulls would be laden with grain as they made their gentle way along the waterways to somewhere like Pell's Mill on the Norfolk bank of the River Waveney at Beccles. A regular motor ship, which Harry remembered, was one called the Halcyon which would mainly run coal for the maltings.

"Well there was this coaster, a motorised barge really, and they wanted what they called a deckie engineer. It was a diesel motor. The Mate was aboard and he say, 'We want someone, what is your experience?

'One Scottish fishing in a drifter.'

'Where from, Yarmouth, Lowestoft?'

I said, 'Lowestoft.'

'Well, I expect the old man will be pleased to see you in the morning when he come back. Come down and see him in the morning.'

"I went down when he said and he signed me straight up. I was with a firm called Metcalfs and all the ships were named after the family, so there was the Taber M, the Charles M and all different names with the M after it. They had a green flag with a white M in the middle. I was to be with the Metcalfs most of my time before the war, mainly on the David M and they kept getting bigger and I finished up in the John M. It was regular work; as soon as we unloaded we sailed again. We used to run to Goole in Yorkshire or Hull to load the coal and then come back, down the Thames, along the coast to Plymouth or the Isle of Wight, all over the place."

Peacetime came to an abrupt halt when the war was declared in September 1939. For one whose working life since the age of 16 had been mainly afloat, firstly with the fishing fleet on the North Sea and then up and down the rivers and along the coast delivering coal and grain, there was no question of joning one of the three main services. Harry's life changed with a natural progression into the Merchant Navy.

"When the war started we were fitted out, putting the machine guns aboard, armaments, and I went to second engineer for a start. Then they sent us as an ammunition supply ship up to Greenock in Scotland. We were off there for about three years… there is a big anchorage off Gorach called the Taylor Bank and all the Navy ships used to come in to anchor and send their ammunition requirements to the office and we would get a message, orders like what they wanted and we used to go out, go alongside and put this ammunition aboard; being an engineer I used to have to drive a winch. We had two soldiers put aboard, a sergeant and an ordinary gunner, two Royal Artillery gunners, and we had twin machine guns plus umpteen other rifles, machine guns and sub-machine-guns. We were all trained, we had to have a turn at it. We were away for about fourteen weeks I think, Scotland and the Shetlands and the Orkneys. The Orkneys were quite a good place because the Yanks were up there, we used to do alright with the Yanks, what with cigarettes and stuff they could get what we couldn't."

Of course it was inevitable that his ship would be involved when the time came to try and get the troops off the beaches at Dunkirk. "We knew what was happening. We knew we were going over to help bring the boys back. That was a funny thing because when we were fitting out for this Dunkirk business we were tied up on the Thames and there was a pub there where we used to go in dinner times and evenings and that. When they found out where we were going, that we were going over to bring the boys back, the landlady, she said, 'By the way, how many in your crew?' 'Well,' we said, 'including the gunners we got thirteen.'

'Thirteen! You can't go to sea with thirteen.'

"We never heard no more for a couple of days, cause we used to go there dinner times when we were stocking up and one thing and another and one dinner time she came out and say, 'You still got thirteen? Here's your fourteenth member.'

"It was a wire-haired terrier pup. That got to be the ship's mascot and it was still abaord when I left the ship. The Skipper took charge of it and when he went home on leave he used to take it with him. He said, 'I can't trust that with you, you'll be drowning it or something.' He was a crazy dog; you know you had your flag at the back, the red ensign, he used to get on the rail and try and catch it, we used to tie the flag to the rail so it didn't flap.

"Early in the morning we went over in a convoy with MTBs and all sorts of drifters, trawlers, armed gun boats, we had a lot with us. The troops were all lined up along the quay and as the ships came in they filled us up. I think it was something like 150–160 we crammed on board. They were standing on the deck, they were down in the engine room, they were everywhere. Everywhere we could get them we got them, some of them only boys you know. They had just about had it, they were sort of at their wits' end some of them were." Harry fell silent for a while. "Some of them were alright. Then when we had taken on board all we could they said, 'Right, off you go,' and we went outside to an anchorage and waited until there were enough for a convoy, then we steamed back. We went across four times. It was only twenty odd miles, should have taken about two hours, but it all depended because we had to do a sort of zig zag course. You couldn't just sail straight over there because there were mine fields and we were being bombed."

Despite his life at sea Harry and Violet's courtship continued and in 1941 he came ashore for a long weekend, Friday to Monday. "We suddenly made up our minds to get married and we went to see the parson in Beccles and explained that I was due back on Monday. He got everything ready and we were married in front of the Sunday School on Sunday morning. I was twenty and Vi about the same. She was in service at the Railway Hotel, they gave us a slap up do they did. I know it was a rushed do but they put on everything, they made a cake and all the rest of it. Yeh, we had a real good time there. Then, course Monday morning I was back on the station at 6 o'clock and on the train. That was my honeymoon!"

Following Dunkirk his ship had returned North. "Yes, we went to Shetland, Lerwick, we were stationed there a time, then from there to the Orkneys for a little while until we finished up in Iceland. They sent us up to Iceland because there were R.A.F. and Army bases up there. They were established up there and had their own canteens which we were invited into. We were taking supplies to them because they had anti-aircraft batteries up there you see, all among the islands. We weren't allowed into the town. We had our own NAAFI near the quay which we could use and the soldiers used that too. The town was out of bounds to us." After a pause… "Nice to look back on."

By 1944 Harry's ship was given orders to once again cross the channel. This time it was a matter of taking over supplies following D-Day. "The beach-head where we went was just a sandy beach with a grass bank and the village a quarter of a mile inland. They laid big wire mesh sheets, steel matting, on the beach; it was a lovely flat beach very similar to Gorleston. Then we went up at high tide and settled on the beach without getting stuck on the sand. They ran the lorries down one side of us, loaded up, then up the other side and away up the beach, away inland with it. It depended on how soon they could get the lorries down. We used to take 700 ton which is several lorry loads! As soon as we were empty we were off back for another load, backwards and forwards. That lasted about a week until they got established enough on shore. They got a couple of ports open so they got the bigger ships going in. A dispatch rider came down to us and said, 'Have you got any white bread? We've been living on hard-tack biscuits for a fortnight ever since we came over here. Do you cook your own bread?' The cook found him a loaf and told him to come back at nine in the morning and there would be another loaf or two for him.

'What do you want for them?'

'We don't want nothing.

"Our cook was a Scotch boy from the Isle of Skye and he was a marvellous cook. Well, he and his mate stayed up all night baking the bread for these squaddies. As soon as the word got round that our cook was baking bread, oh dear, they come round…They come down about three mornings whilst we were there. The first time they ran out of flour, so the next time we went away he say, 'I'll make sure I have enough flour if we go back,' which we did."

At that time before the war when Harry had given his notice in at the fruit farm his employer had unsuccessfully tried to persuade him from going to sea. Now, at the end of the war, he reflected on that decision without any regrets. "It was the best thing I done, it kept me out of the forces during the war. We were a reserved occupation in the Merchant Navy. Mind you we had to go where we were told. All the while, right until I packed up after the war, I was with just one motor coaster firm. When I told them I was going to pack up and go ashore they say, 'You're doing wrong you know.' and I say, 'I'll have to take a chance on that.'" Once again Harry could say, "I never regretted it, I spent all the time with Vi."

* * *

Harry considered himself fortunate in spending the war in the Merchant Navy rather than the armed forces. Certainly as a professional seaman he was much more at home on board his ship than many who suddenly found themselves in the Royal Navy without any experience and without doubt he enjoyed much of his time spent at sea. However, just between September 1939 and May 1940 the Merchant Navy took a severe battering; 177 Merchant ships were sunk during that period. In fact the Register of Shipping and Seamen records that of the 185,000 men and women who served in the

Merchant Navy during the Second World War, 36,749 were lost by enemy action. 5,720 were taken prisoner and 4,707 were wounded, totaling 47,176 casualties – that is 27% of their number.

They are remembered in the Merchant Navy Association Prayer:

> On all the oceans white cap flow,
> You do not see crosses row on row
> But those who sleep beneath the sea,
> Rest in peace for your country's free.

In gratitude and to the memory of the Merchant Navy Seafarers of all the allied countries who sacrificed their lives during WWII.

> May they rest in peace
> In God's good keeping.

(To be seen in St. Paul's Anglican Pro-Cathedral, Valletta, Malta)

3
IVAN AND SYLVIA
THE START OF A LONG AND HAPPY MARRIAGE

The police constable in the East Suffolk village of Wenhaston was transferred to a similar village post in Ringsfield, just a few miles from the market town of Beccles. It was 1929 and the constable and his wife had a six year old daughter and a young son of just three. They were to be there for the remainder of son Ivan's childhood and throughout the war which was then barely on the horizon. Their home, which was also the police station, was a house rented by the force in the centre of the village. By the time it came for Ivan's father to retire he had bought it, paying £225 for the house and part of the orchard and later a further £25 for the other half of the orchard, land that is still in the family to this day. Consequently a new house was built as an official police station when the next officer moved to the village.

"When we come to live in the village there were very few houses and on that road the very last property was the village shop run by Mr B., the retired village policeman. That had practically everything you needed really, they sold a little of everything, including paraffin, and you could go to the back door and get vinegar on a Sunday.

"There was just my older sister and me. In 1929 they had

just built the new school, because I've got an idea that my sister might have gone to the old school for a while."

So Ivan was fortunate in living in a comfortable home with a bed to himself and the school just a few steps along the road. At about the time that Ivan arrived in Ringsfield Sylvia was born in Loddon, between Beccles and Norwich. Soon, her father, a painter and decorator by trade, managed to find work in Redisham and promptly moved his family to this small village just a few miles from Ringsfield.

"We were in a little house in Redisham, there were ten of us in three bedrooms. When the time came we had to walk to Ilketshall St. Lawrence School. That's a long walk [nearly two miles] and we used to take Veronica, she was just old enough to start school and we used to push her with a cansard [a type of pushchair]." Sylvia is a small person, so in those days she must have been tiny. The walk to school, pushing her sister, must have been very challenging for little legs.

"Mother used to cut up our lunch, I think that used to be a couple of rounds of bread and something, and they'd got a ditch in their playing field and we used to sit in the ditch and eat our dinner in good weather. Sometimes we used to eat the food before dinner time. You walked to school, you were hungry! I think there were two teachers, Mr Walker, the headmaster, and a lady teacher.

"I weren't very old when I went to Redisham, but I must have been six or seven when I come to Ringsfield. That's when the council houses were built and the first three houses were four-bedroomed and we had the first one. There were mother and father and eight children. I can remember coming there and I was only allowed to push the baby up and down as far as the shop whilst they were moving the furniture and putting the beds and everything up. Dad died when Mum was 36 yrs. and left her with eight children to bring up. The eldest was fourteen and Maureen, the youngest was two."

"You must have been about ten when your father died. Sylvia is three years younger than me."

"There were mainly large families, I wouldn't say there was actual poverty, but there wasn't much to spare. When Father died Mother used to get 10/- [50p] a week for herself and half-a-crown [12 ½ p] for each child; that was called Parish Relief in those days."

During that era between the wars if you lived in the towns, particularly those along the coast such as Gt.Yarmouth you would have been accustomed to various street traders each with their own distinctive cry, "Cromer Crabs. Fine Cromer Crabs", the starting price of a crab ? just 6d [2 ½p], "Apples, pears, cherries – muscatel and almonds" – always ending in a high pitched crescendo of "All ripe and juicy!" and "Lovely Williams! Sweet Williams!" – baskets of large juicy pears, so succulent that the juice used to drop into your ears. In the countryside however, in a good season fruit was plentiful and although they did not enjoy these particular characters the village was reasonably self-sufficient and was well served by a number of delivery men, first with horses and carts and then with vans, coming out from the nearby market town. There was certainly a fishmonger, who with his horse and cart went to Lowestoft fish market and then plied his trade around the town and the surrounding district. A number of coal merchants delivered regularly, one, who Sylvia remembers, always had two men in the cab and one standing on the back. Then there was the oil man. Coal, oil and paraffin, three necessities in a time when electricity had not reached the village and central heating was something for the future. A welcome caller for all the family and particularly the children was 'the Corona man'. From the 1920s the Corona pop man with his horse and cart delivered those special bottles of coloured fizzy drink: orangeade, limeade and cherryade to start with and then more exotic flavours. Each bottle was cleverly designed with a glass marble, a rubber washer and a swing top that forced the marble into the neck of the bottle, ensuring that the fizz didn't escape. Better still, proving that recycling is nothing new, the children would collect the empty bottles and earn a few pennies when they returned them to the delivery man. Other ways of augmenting meagre earnings would be selling rabbit skins at 3d [1p] each to the rag and bone man, and in the early years of the war a local Young Farmers Club organised sparrow killings offering ½ d for each dead bird in an attempt to protect the food supply; such a menace were the large flocks on the farms. The shop met many of the community's other needs and then there was the Post Office. "The Post Mistress was a stern one, you had to mind your ps and qs when you went in there."

The conversation of couples who have not only grown up together in the same small community and have then enjoyed a long happily married life tends to blend into one as they feed each other's memories. As one draws breath the other chips in sharing with us a vivid picture of their childhood in a 1930s rural Suffolk village. Sylvia is the first to reminisce by recalling the laundry which employed quite a number of women.

"You would go in one building and there would be all the women with baths, pumping up and down, washing things, I didn't see them use a dolly, perhaps they had scrub boards. Then, after they had rinsed them there were big old mangles going, then there would be rows and rows hung outside, they used to dry outside. Then in the other place there would be a sort of huge stove with a fire in the bottom and the irons heating. There must have been ten women working there at least. A man used to go round Beccles collecting all the laundry. When they rinsed the washing they always had to rinse them in water dyed blue, and you had this little cube of blue tied up in a piece of muslin, and you would dip that in your cold water, and that had to be blue because that made the things white. I remember one woman what worked there and someone asked her about her job and she said, 'It's a bloomin' sight harder than being in the workhouse!'"

However, it was their childhood activities which they particularly enjoyed re-living as there was always something to do.

"We'd go fishing a lot, in ponds. There were fish in most of the ponds and there were a lot of ponds which are not there now. There was a big pond in a meadow called the Leys and you'd get boys all round that with their fishing rods. On the opposite side of the road there were two other ponds and some of the fish were golden carp; we'd take them home and put them in a jar or something, poor little 'ol things. We'd go out on the farms in the summertime and help in the harvest fields."

"We didn't do that as much as the boys but it was fun at thrashing time. When the thrashing machine came round the farms, oh that was great excitement. You'd take your jam jar and catch the little mice when they started thrashing."

The farms were natural playgrounds and Sylvia was a real tomboy, jumping hedges, climbing trees and jumping from one haystack to another.

"During the summer holidays we used to walk right round St.Lawrence, a gang of twelve of us, just go for a walk. You didn't worry if you missed a meal, you never thought about it. You had probably had your breakfast and you wouldn't be home any more until 4 o'clock, something like that. Just playing outside. Mrs Stannard lived on the corner, if she caught you on the village pump, coo dear! We used to have about fourteen buckets of water, more on a wash day. We used to give each other a ride on the pump, push it up and let the wheel come down with the person sitting on the handle. Big 'ol wheel. That was big, huge – iron weren't it ? Old Mrs Stannard used to sit up in her bedroom window and she'd tap on the window. It used to get a bit dry in the summertime and that would come out chalky, coo we used to get into trouble, she used to blame everyone for that. Other times during the school holidays we used to play Mothers and Fathers; and we used to have a peg and put an apple on for a head and have little bits of material to make little dresses and things for our peg doll. Then there was maidenhair, I think you called it, the grass, and we used to get all different coloured silver paper and put a little piece on each grass and give them to our parents to put in a vase." Childhood memories came flooding back to Sylvia – "And we used to make hairbands out of – what do you call it, Ivan? – it was like the greaseproof paper we have in cornflakes, and somehow we used to plait them and make hairbands. When you think about it, if the children wanted something to write on, nobody bought any paper, there was always a tea packet or a sugar bag. There were a lot of us, we never had writing paper to do any writing for school, a lot of the time they gave us little made-up notebooks. When I first started school the young ones had slate boards to write on. Good old days! The children enjoyed their childhood in those days."

"And you never heard a child say they were bored, did you? That wasn't even thought of. If you hadn't anything to do your parents soon found something for you to do! If you had gone and said you were bored you would be working full time! During the war on that little corner plot they used to have an old cart what they used to pull into the road to stop the traffic. When they thought there was going to be an invasion they got road blocks and things you see, they got some old carts and all sorts of things. There was that old wagon cart and the kids used to love playing in that. There were two wooden snow ploughs in the village, children always played on them in the summertime. Come the snow they put the horses on the front, there weren't many tractors in those days, they only had horses. Of course, the blacksmith was there, so the children used to love going up and watching him shoeing the horses. The cry would go up, 'There's some horses gone up for horse shoes, come on let's go and see.' He had big doors open toward the road, and he used to take the horses in there or sometimes he would shoe them outside. Oh yes, we used to spend hours up there. When you think, was it Longfellow? 'Under The Spreading Chestnut Tree.' – and it's dead right with the children watching and the sparks flying. And right in front of the blacksmith's was a big sandstone on a wheel. The carpenter was Mr Norman, he'd be the next house along, and sometimes you would see him with a hose and things sharpening them up on the sandstone. And shears, yes anything like that, we kids would like to go and help turn the wheel. That was a big wheel, a gigantic thing; I expect that stood six feet high."

"Children don't know half do they? There was a lot going on, different things. Tell you one of the things the parents didn't like that we did – Mr Springall had a bull and if we saw someone take a cow down to Mr Springall's bull, the kids used to like to sit on the gate and cheer. Of course, we all kept rabbits, so that's how we got to know the facts of life, because you were never told, you must never speak of anything like that, EVER. We used to catch the wild rabbits, take them home and put them in a hutch. Someone complained and reported it to Ivan's father, the policeman, so he come and opened all the cages and just let them out on Mr Merrell's field. Then Mr Merrells complained!

"Merrells had a pond on their farm and we used to go down there and paddle, and the cows used to walk into it and mess as well. Of course, the Hundred River was a great attraction, all the childen used to go and play down there. You could jump the river in places where it weren't too wide and you could paddle and get your feet wet when you weren't supposed to with your shoes on. You'd take your socks off and thrash them on the road and put them on again. They were all large families in the four council houses, so we always had someone to play with. You would play all sorts of games on the road; we'd chalk to play hop scotch, and we used to have hoops didn't we? Skipping ropes. Part of the year would be tops, it used to go in seasons – conkers. Boys used to have a snail race; used to catch the snails and make a little square in the road with dirt round, so that was their dirt track and then they used to put lanes in for the races."

It was a rural community, most working on the land with hard and long hours. However, the adults were not without their own form of relaxation as there was an old quoit house, a little stone building of big flints and a square piece of land near the village pump where many a game was played. Quoits was not a game of hoop-la played with horseshoes. The quoits were rings of steel, dished one side and curved the other, each weighing about 3½ lbs. There were strict rules as to where the pins were put and how the quoits were thrown and placed near them. A summer evening's game, approved by the church as it kept the men out of the pub.

When Ivan was old enough he went straight to the village school. "That was a church school, actually it was pretty good for a village school. By the time I went Mrs White was there, we used to call her Granny White, she used to cycle from Beccles on an old high nelly bike if you know what I mean, she rode real up straight and wore a long black skirt."

"You had to be well behaved, Mrs White had a cane and she washed Kenny Walker's mouth out with carbolic soap because he swore in the playground. Little Kenny, bless his heart, he lived with his Grandma down Poll's Lane, in a caravan. He used to wear droopy trousers and we all cheeked him, didn't we. I can picture poor little Kenny now, his Grandma used to bring him to school, 'course they wore black skirts down to the ankle, great heavy skirts all the year round."

"I did quite well there," Ivan reflected upon his school years, "and when you reached ten or eleven you had to go to the Beccles Council School but I had been in a class of children older than me and I wasn't allowed to go with the others to Beccles, so when I did go I came first in the class every time. I was good at Maths, I could spell but I was not good at English. I cycled to school and then, of course, in '39 the Area Modern School opened so we went there. It wasn't long before war broke out, so we used to go mornings and the evacuees went in the afternoons. That was fine that was! We thought that was marvellous, school from 8 a.m – 1 p.m."

When Sylvia followed in his footsteps three years later the education authority, "provided us all with a bicycle and sou'westers, your waterproof and cape which had a sort of loop so you could put it on your handlebars, and leggings. By the time it had come to my sister Maureen that had all finished and she had to walk from Ringsfield to the Area

Modern School. There was no other means of getting there. I left school at fourteen and went into a lady's house as nursing maid. I bathed a new born baby at fourteen. First I did the post round, then I went nursemaiding, but then Mum wasn't very well so I went home to the family and when she got better I got the job at the Post Office which was £1 a week and that was a bit more than I was getting nursemaiding."

The suggestion that there may have been any crime in the village was met by Ivan with a wry chuckle. "Riding cycles without lights! I can remember my father during the war when he had special constables and he had to run the air raid wardens into Beccles and the special constable used to bring someone round the house who he had just stopped for riding without lights or something like that. My father would give them a ticking off and let them go and when they had disappeared he'd turn to the special, 'What did you bring them for? Think of all the paperwork!' He didn't like paperwork. When you think about it, when we first went to the village there were no telephones you see, so he used to get his orders in the Police Gazette and they used to come through the post every day. He hardly used to look at these papers. In that old house there were piles of paperwork which went back with the police for years. In this *Police Gazette* that told you all the different crimes that had been happening. At one time I used to do the paperwork for him, I was only young at school but I didn't mind doing something like that. You'd get these papers and then you would go to another one and it would give you a number and other information, then you would check back and if the person had been arrested you would write 'Arrested' across it. I used to enjoy doing it really."

The *Police Gazette*, also known rather aptly as The Hue and Cry provided weekly information and daily supplements about the various crimes ranging from housebreaking, robbery and arson to stolen horses and livestock, and murder, as well as information about deserters from the armed forces. There were pictures of known criminals and sometimes rewards offered for information. For a young schoolboy this must have been as exciting as the weekly comic.

"And then in about, I don't know what the year would be, they installed a telephone. Of course, that was a marvellous thing because the only other telephone in the village was at the Post Office. So they had to put a set of poles down specially for our telephone. The lady in the telephone exchange used to ring the bell every morning and that used to be just testing the line. She gave a certain ring so my sister and I would nearly fight each other to see who could answer first.'Course that was on the wall so we had to stand on a chair to reach it. The number was 46, then it was 146, then 3146. Then Mr Ulph got a telephone and his number was 183. During the war you see every time there was an air raid warning or something like that they phoned through to the Police Station and if my Father weren't there one of us would answer it. If it was air raid warning Yellow there was a possibility ; if it was air raid warning Red that was supposed to be imminent. One night we got bombed. The bomb fell in the field where the village green is now; we had five bombs in that field. I was indoors and I heard this plane coming over, this bomb came down and I thought the door was coming in. I dived under the table and my Mother was in the hall, she came crawling on her hands and knees, my Father wasn't at home. Glass didn't break, but the bedroom ceiling come down but not straight away; the bomb had gone off, the planes had gone and all of a sudden there was a crash two or three minutes afterwards, and there was a big lump, I suppose about six feet square, because in those days they were old plaster and straw ceilings and the whole lot come down. That was a tidy mess. In the morning, myself and most of the other young boys were going over there looking for bits of shrapnel and they found there was an unexploded bomb there, so we were turned off right quick. I was at school then and there was this explosion and they had taken it out and down to the sand pit near Alexander's Farm and blew it up in the pit."

"The airman died didn't he, Ivan?"

"That was later when the Americans were here. Anybody who saw the American planes will never see the like again. They used to go out, they used to be flying round and round getting into formation, from all the airdromes round here. They'd go out 500 bombers at a time and there used to be one plane yellow and black who used to be the one to get them into formation. He'd get planes from one airdrome up and then he'd get another lot, bring them all round and they'd all go out together. The noise you can imagine can't you 400 – 500 bombers going round. Coo... that was incredible really. The British went out at night and the Americans used to be the daylight bombers. On this occasion they came back late, perhaps they were long in getting ready to go out, or they went a bit further and for whatever reason they came back in the dark and were flying round with all the landing lights on, it was crazy really. Some of the airfields didn't like to put the airfield lights on they said, and some crashed on landing. As the Americans came in some German fighters came with them and shot them down all round here, they lost fifteen bombers that night round this area. One of them came down at Barsham. That night I'd been to somewhere Geldeston way and I was biking home the other side of the river like and I actually saw the tracer bullets hit that plane. You could see 'em fly and you heard the guns and wonder what's going on really. I see these tracers in the sky and didn't know what they were and then all of a sudden there was such a roar and that come straight down on the ground. When I got home everybody was out, they found three American airmen, there had been eleven in the plane and these three had parachuted out into the wood near us. They said there was another parachute so there would be another man somewhere. We spent nearly all night, well a long while, looking for him. Then I went to bed and just as it was getting light in the morning someone came along and said there was something in the field up near the Post Office. I went up with my Father and there was the airman who had parachuted and it had burnt off his back, you could see where it had burnt through and he had landed face down in that field. His name was Hook and he came from Massachusetts, because he'd got his name on his tag. That stick in the mind. They reckon they lost fifteen that night. Eleven men in each. But you don't know how many had been lost before they got home do you? That was a terrible night.

"I went down and looked at the plane the next morning and it was just a churned up field, smoking. The tail had come off and that was in the field the other side of the road. There was no guard on the plane, and one of my mates, well two of them, they must have been 16 or 17, the plane had twin machine guns and they pinched one of them. Took it home and put it in the shed. In them days you got no end of old bullets, so they got some of them and took it on the common. They couldn't get it to repeat, but they got it to fire. Then Bobby's father found it, coo, he nearly went mad. Bobby got into real trouble over that. His father took it and they reckon that he threw it in a dyke on the marshes. I know my Father was on about it, I daren't tell him where it was!"

One crime that Ivan's Father did deal with was when a group of soldiers who were billeted at Redisham Hall had a night out and on their way home they swung on the sign post and broke it. "It was one of the old ones for when they had coaches, so it was right high. Being the policeman he went up to the Hall and consequently half a dozen soldiers were sent to dig a hole and put it in again so it became a short sign post!"

The old village hall was wooden structure and this together with the pub were the social centres for the community; there were darts matches and at one time Ivan was in charge of the young boys as there was a young men's club. There were socials and dances, and it was one night after a dance that Ivan walked Sylvia home, tall thin Ivan with little Sylvia barely coming up to his shoulder. This was to be the beginning of a relationship that was to blossom into a long and happy marriage.

"I went out with him just before I was 18, he was three years older, engaged at 19 and married at 23. 'Cause I couldn't get married before because I had to pay for my own wedding."

"And we couldn't get a house anyway, that was the biggest problem."

They were married for 66 years, brought up a family of boys, were an essential part of their grandchildren's lives, much loved by them all, but there begins another story.

4
SAM

Meet Sam – rosy cheeked, soft of voice, short of stature and a bit tubby. He came into the world in 1909 before the rumblings of the great catastrophe that was to follow. It was a period when for decades very little had altered in the rural areas; it was only with the Great War that life began to change radically. For the moment, though, horses were used to plough the fields, horses provided most of the road transport and the status quo remained very much as it had always been.

The family lived in Lowestoft where Sam's Father worked as a butcher. With a wife and four other mouths to feed; for there was Sam, the eldest boy, with a brother and two sisters, his wage would have barely stretched sufficiently to meet all their needs. Then came the crisis when war was declared and he was called up – or was he? Initially recruitment was voluntary and the drive to encourage men to enlist entailed over 54 million posters with that famous one of Kitchener's pointing finger and the slogan 'Your Country Needs You!'; then there was the picture of a family by their fireside with the children asking their Father 'What Did You Do In The War Daddy?'. Letters were sent out to thousands of households, speeches were made in towns throughout the land. There was a huge wave of patriotic fervour and a sense of duty to the King and the Empire. It was not until January 1916 that the first Military Service Act introduced conscription for single men of military age, closely followed on 25th May of that year by the second Act which included married men. However long before he was obliged to do so Sam's Father joined up and his Mother would have to try and manage on the little that was allowed for families left at home. The pre-war average weekly wage varied from between 26s 4d and 34s 4d [£1 32p – £1 72p]. A new private in the army would receive the basic rate of just 1s 1d a day; at home the wife's separation allowance was 7s 7d plus 1s 2d per child and if her husband died then she would receive a maximum pension of 10s [50p] a week. Certainly it was the widely held concern that led to a number of debates in Parliament about the hardship incurred and a push for better rates of pay.

Why did he enlist? We shall never know. How was the family to manage? Part of the answer came in a lifeline following a visit from Sam's Mother's brother and his wife who were tenant farmers in Worlingham just outside Beccles. On hearing of their brother-in-law's call-up they went post-haste to visit the Lowestoft family. They obviously had a plan for as they left their parting words were, "We'll take your eldest boy and keep him until the war is over or his Father comes home." This was too good an offer to turn down and arrangements were quickly made for Sam's Mother to deliver him to the farm the very next day. These were still the days of the carriers, who, with their horses and wagon, provided regular transport and a delivery service between the towns and villages. In Beccles John Cousins made twice weekly trips to Norwich and back and the one we are interested in would have been Mr William Clarke, who every Wednesday and Saturday left Beccles for the Blue Inn Yard in Lowestoft, picking up people and parcels along the way. His wife would often join him with a shopping list from various folk, usually for items from the Maypole Store, a shop which would only be found in the larger towns. The Maypole Dairy Company had started life as a family grocery business in Wolverhampton in 1887, joining forces with another company six years later. It specialised in butter and margarine and a range of basic working class staple goods. By 1913 it had 800 branches throughout the country, its success due largely to the growing popularity of margarine. Back to Sam: that day he was told they were off to visit his Uncle Billy. It was with great excitement the five year old and his Mother watched the horses being taken out of the stables and put into their harnesses before they climbed onto the carrier's wagon for its return journey from the Blue Inn yard. Sam had a vivid memory of what happens next.

"When we got to the bottom of Rectory Lane they pulled up and Mother say, 'Come on, we're going to see Uncle Billy now.' Well, I thought this was a great idea. My aunt heard the horses and is coming into the lane to meet us. 'Come on,' she say, 'come on and see what I have got for you.'"

Sam didn't look back as he followed his aunt and so didn't see his Mother return to the wagon to go into the town in time to catch the train back to Lowestoft without him. Unaware of his Mother's departure Sam settled down to play with the toys Aunt Gertie produced out of a cupboard. By the time his Uncle Billy arrived home from the farm, the boy, worn out by a long and exciting day, was asleep on the floor and was promptly scooped up and put to bed.

So began Sam's new life which, obviously to start with, was very confusing. Unbeknown to him his aunt and uncle had a lodger so the next morning being Sunday he was dressed in a new suit and this stranger took him off to church. This was a totally new experience for him and the long sermon proved too much for Sam who nodded off, leaning onto this woman's arm. As they left the church porch behind them he was firmly told, "I shall bring a pin the next time and instead of nipping you I shall prick you." Sam's response – "I didn't think much of this and kept awake after that. I always sat with her, morning and evening service until I was old enough to join the choir when I was eleven."

Confusion compounded confusion; still without any explanation the same woman took his hand the following day and took him to school. It became apparent that she was the headmistress of the village primary school and he was to go on to have a happy relationship with her as did most of the other children; she was much loved and to this day is remembered with great affection.

"I was handed over to the teacher of the infants' class in the small room. The lady who had brought me went through to the larger room where she taught the top classes."

He settled into a happy school life, doing well and showing promise; however life in the farmhouse was not so easy and he was soon set to do various chores. "When I was about 7 yrs. old my uncle said, 'Come on now, you are getting a big boy, you eat a lot and cost a lot to keep. You get up when I call you and come to the farm to do some work.' Before this I had to go to the Rectory nearby to clean shoes every morning and fill the coal scuttles with coal from the cellar down under the house. Two evenings a week I had to pump water by a horse pump to fill a tank situated in the attic up in the roof; this supplied all the needs of water through the house."

However now his Uncle wanted Sam to work on the farm before and after school and then Saturdays and Sunday mornings before church. This was the era when everyone went to church unless they were unwell.

Sam continues, "This was before breakfast, then on the way to school I would deliver milk to one or two people and then pick up the empty milk cans on the way home in the afternoon, then work until tea time and agin in the light evenings until it got dark. I always remember the first time he put me to a cow; he put me to a cow which would accept me, an old cow you could do anything with and it was right warm and I fell asleep before I'd finished milking. Never dared let him know. I didn't know any other sort of life but he was a cruel old beggar, or my Aunt was, because if I wasn't home from school by a certain time she would call, 'That boy i'nt home yet, go on arter him.' Now he never hit a horse with a stick or whip but he always had a whip standing handy and he would come and meet me out of school and he would catch me unawares sometimes and didn't I know it. Because you see I would hang around with the other boys after school for a little while and when I went to collect the empty milk cans if their children were there playing down in the garden or in the yard I would go and see what they were doing and that's how the time was doing. These mothers would always give me the down if they saw him. I always remember being at the bottom of the garden with one of them there and he came round to see where I was and she daren't call because he had already passed her and was coming down the path and as soon as I saw him I jumped up you see 'cause he slashed his whip and down I went. She had a man dig her garden because her husband was called up, gone away as a soldier in '14 War, and I fell on the edge; of course she didn't want to get onto me, but she wanted to get onto him for knocking me down and spoiling the edge of her path. But I was the one that got wrong for it though." [Aren't children always keenly aware of such injustices and they are not forgotten even after a long life?] "They even hid me up sometimes in their kitchens till he had gone past. Even the policeman was afraid of him. I used to call at theirs for the milk can and his wife has hidden me up in her room if he's coming that way looking for me. Then I would get home before him. He would be as riled as anything to think he had missed me.

"I loved working with horses. One day we finished school early for the harvest holiday and Uncle called me. He'd only got one horse then and I knew he got it fixed to the plough.

He said 'Come on boy, come along wi' me.'
I said 'Where are we going?'
'You come along wi' me and you'll see.'
'What am I going to do?'
'I'll shew you.'
"He was Jack Blunt like that. So I got there (to the field) and I watched him. He stepped out in the little field where the church hall now stands, he strided out so far and put in a stake at the bottom, half way again... I was standing here with the horse...he got the horse to draw a furrow down there in line with those two sticks, he came back again and the old horse came round again in the furrow.

'There you are boy,' he say, 'keep the plough up straight, the old horse know what to do.'

"I was eight years old. So I kept going down and up, down and up, till I got to the Church wall, couldn't go any further, cause there was this lot done going down and this lot down coming back. He was across the field doing some hoeing, so I called 'Uncle Billy!'

'What you want?'
'I want another furra.'
'Alright.' So away he come, he stepped out again from that last furrow between the sticks, one down there, one the middle and then come and got in line and he drew another furrow, down and back. 'There you are boy, that'll keep you going.'

'Right. Thank you.' and I keep going and going, until I catch up again. So I call again.

'What der you want?' I said I wanted another furra. 'Well you'll have to do it yourself I can't keep running arter you.'

"So I thought 'Right'. I knew what he'd done, so I went and stepped out and put the sticks in. I'll tell you something, I learnt my biggest lesson, because when I got to that first stick you should keep your eye on the other one and keep going, don't stop for nothing if you don't have to, don't take your eye off. Well, I stopped. I wanted to look back to see how well I'd come, and it was perfect, perfect that far and I touched the reins of the old horse and said, 'Come on old gall'. When I got to the bottom I turned round and looked again, but oh dear, from here to there I'd taken my eye off the marker in line with that one and I'd gone round to it. That meant that when I went back on this side I had to take it a little wider till I got to where it was alright and when I came this side I had to narrow this side a bit till I got it perfect again. That was alright. I was reading my little Bible one day and what do you think the verse was I came across? 'He that putteth his hand to the plough and looketh back is not fit for the Kingdom of Heaven.' Coo, I'll never go to heaven, I looked back. And you know that stuck with me. Yes, 'cause I thought I was a good boy seeing I went to church you see.

"When the harvest holiday was over it was back to school but I used to have to go up to the farm early morning with him to help with the cleaning up and the milking and back again after school; there was all the preparing of the food ready for the cows, quite a lot to do. When I wasn't doing that I was doing gardening. I got a shilling a week, most of that was by 3d here and 3d there, where on the way to school I took the milk because they hadn't got anyone to send, in some cases the man was away in the war. When I was delivering milk it was alright, but when I was working on the farm my Aunt could not bear to hear me whistling and I was always whistling. Of course I had to hand my money over to her and she said, 'Every time I catch you whistling I shall take a penny out of your money.' Sometimes I got no money at all at the end of the week. So I stopped whistling and I got my full money of a shilling at the end of the week. One day I started whistling again and she said, 'You're at it again, it'll be tuppence every time.' I found my shilling didn't last very long so I had to give up whistling altogether."

During this time, when Sam had been with his Aunt and Uncle for a couple of years or so, they got a letter to say that Sam's Father had been wounded and had been sent home. Uncle Billy had gone to work so Aunt Gertie opened the letter and was delighted at the thought of getting rid of the boy, the agreement having been to keep him until his Father came home. She obviously hadn't wanted him in the first place. Without more ado Sam was taken home to his family.

"Of course, when Uncle came home and come up to the table at meal time, there's no place set for me. He said 'Where's the boy?'

She said, 'I took him home. His father's home and that's what we agreed.'

"He never said a word, he drew away from the table, he didn't touch his food or drink. He sat for a while and he got up and went off to the farm, which was up the road. He came back at night with the night milk and then went back to the farm till dark when he came home and went to bed. He still didn't eat any food at home or speak. This went on for three days and after he went to work Aunt said to herself, 'I can't stick this any longer I must go and fetch the boy.' So, on her bike she came over to Lowestoft; Mother was pleased to see her and wondered why and was told, 'I've come after that boy because Billy 'ont eat nor speak.'

"Mother called me and said, 'Come on you are going to see your uncle.' That was all that was said and he was pleased enough when he came home and found I was there and life started again."

The routine of school and farm work continued for Sam but it was not without its ups and downs for the household. The farm his uncle worked did not have a house attached to it so they rented a house nearby in Rectory Lane from another farmer until the owner wanted it for his farm steward. They had to up sticks and move to Poultry Farm which had some nice buildings so they were able to keep chickens, another job for Sam along with a bit of gardening. Another move came when that house was needed for a new cowman. This time there wasn't another house readily available so Uncle Billy approached a local builder with the idea of having a house built on the farm. It was agreed that they would move into part of the builder's house for the interim, something which Sam particularly enjoyed as it meant that he had other children to play with. Things were not to go according to plan though; the war was on and there was urgent building work to be done in the district so it not being a priority work on the house came to a standstill. Sam's Uncle Billy, being both an impatient and intolerant man, consequently gave the builder an ultimatum, 'Get the job done or clear up the mess!' The building work was jettisoned and the family given notice to quit their lodgings. For a while life became more uncomfortable for Sam; he had now lost the friends he played with. His uncle bought two caravans, one to live in and one to sleep in, putting them in a meadow adjacent to the farm buildings and at night Sam was sent to clamber into his bunk early so that he would be asleep when his aunt and uncle turned in. Fortunately some time after this the council bought an acre of the land to build four houses. His uncle applied and was promised the first one to be completed and, once again, Sam was to have his own bedroom.

In those days Worlingham was a small village with about thirty families, not the suburb of Beccles which it is now with a population of nearly four thousand and growing. In 1901 there were just 181 folk, nearly all of whom depended upon the land in one way or another for their living. Of course up at the Hall they employed a number of domestic staff, a laundry woman, gamekeeper and an estate carpenter, but the other villagers were mainly farmers together with a market gardener, a marshman and of course the mainstay of such a community, one man who was both blacksmith and wheelwright. The village supported an elementary school which could take up to seventy children although in Sam's day the average attendance was in the region of fifty eight. Opposite the school stood the Worlingham Oak which you will see on the village sign today, where it was reputed that an old man used to sit in the hollow of the tree cobbling shoes. He was, in fact, the postman who walked in with the post in the morning, sat cobbling all day before returning to Beccles with the post in the evening. Sam heard this story and used to prowl around the tree looking for evidence of its former occupant. The postman in Sam's childhood had been issued with a bicycle and used to cycle out through the various villages before settling down in a little shed which he had in Worlingham where he sat and repaired shoes. People brought their shoes to him and would usually pick them up the same day or at a pre-arranged time the next day. Then he would lock up around 4 o'clock and cycle back to the town emptying the postboxes on his way.

One of the most vivid memories Sam had concerning the great oak was from that war time period. A large military park had been established on the land adjacent to the drive leading to Worlingham Hall. The Denbighshire Royal Horse Artillery were billeted on nearby Beccles Common and on the Park at Worlingham. What was possibly a YMCA hut was built at Worlingham at the cost of £750 [£45,000 in today's money]. As most of the men were accommodated in tents, this hut provided a little comfort during the winter months where the soldiers would find refreshments, newpapers and writing materials. Many of these extra comforts were provided by donations from the local population who also sent out Concert Parties to entertain the troops. The day that was so memorable to Sam was July 26th 1916. King George V came to inspect the troops. Crowds lined the streets in Beccles and on the road out to the village. At the King's request there were no church bells rung, which would normally herald a royal visit, and no cheering. It was said that the silence was a moving feature of the visit, but what excitement for a small boy.

Sam continues, "I was only a boy and I came running across the field at the back of the church right down to the corner opposite where the village sign now stands and watched and saw them, saw the troops come by. I saw the King. He didn't take any notice of me!"

The King took the salute standing beneath the great Worlingham Oak.

Sadly, some years later the farmer on whose land the tree stood brought in steam engines to work the land instead of horses. "Big old steam engines, they came in pairs. There was one at each side of the field and they had a long cable, a man would be riding on it with a multi-furrow balance plough, two or three furrows at a time and when it got there it switched off and the other one started. He'd move a little way and he would pull it back and that's how they ploughed. The farmer said, 'That tree's in the way,' because it wasn't in the hedge, it was in the corner of the field. Now, with the horses they used to go round it and when these steam engines came into being they had the tree down. Everybody was very upset about it; they didn't know about it until it was done. Very upset. It was history you see, it was where King George V stood when he viewed the troops as they marched by."

The years at the small Worlingham school were happy ones. "I liked school. I was skipping some classes, just swallowing them up. I started off in the infants, the babies, There were infants and then there was Class 1 and Class 2, then you went in the next room and started with Standard 1 and Standard 2. We used a slate mostly." The Headmistress wanted Sam to go to the secondary school in the town and Sam was certainly keen to do so but his uncle had other ideas and when Sam reached his thirteenth birthday he had no option but to leave school and start work full time.

"Old Mr Self had a dairy in Beccles and he used to take our milk and then it got that there wasn't enough for him and he had to find another supplier. That's when I started going round with the milk because we had got a surplus. It meant that there was the morning's milk; my Aunt used to put it on a tray and scoop the cream off and save that till the end of the week to make butter. I used to take the afternoon round because to start with I was still at school. I went round the village with a wheelbarrow and a little churn of milk and serving cans of measures of ½ pint and 1 pint and went from door to door about tea time. Nearly every house bought milk off me. There were one or two who worked on the farms where they had got cows and they were allowed a pint a day to take home."

There was still a surplus of milk and butter so Sam's Uncle bought a pony and cart and started to build up a milk round in Beccles offering milk at ½ d cheaper than the other people and soon got enough customers. "That caused a bit of a rumpus but he told them that when they brought their price down we shall all be alike and that's what happened. The price of milk in those days was 2½d in winter and 2d in summer."

"There were some Salvation Army people lived in the village at this time. Their meeting place was a hall in Northgate in Beccles. The Wilsons, they lived at Hall Farm and everyone

called Mr Wilson 'Sunshine'. Whenever you saw him he had a big smile and a word for everybody. When he died everyone in the village was sad, even us youngsters. Living in Worlingham, he was buried in Worlingham Churchyard. The Salvation Army Band from Beccles went down to Hall Farm and led the hearse through the village to the churchyard. All were gathered round the grave; I think everybody that posssibly could be from the village was there too. I believe I heard the vicar say that because he was a Salvationist he is not allowed to be brought into the church for a service. So they had a service round the grave. I was watching from the other side of the church wall. Afterwards, the Officer who had conducted the service said, 'There will be a memorial service to our brother at the Salvation Hall tomorrow evening for anybody who wants to come.' That would be the Sunday evening. Uncle Billy was standing by the Officer as he was the Sexton and had been responsible for preparing the grave and for attending to it afterwards and this was when I generally helped. Even during my school days I helped him because in those days funerals had to be on Saturdays. The undertaker did not have many pall bearers because the men who done this usually worked on the farms and they were only free for funerals on their Saturday afternoon off. That evening Uncle said he would like to go to Sunshine's Memorial Service and Aunt Gertie said she would come too. I said I would like to come but was told, 'No, you are in the choir and must go to church.' So, that's what happened. Nobody asked me at church, 'Where's uncle tonight?' During their summer months with light evenings the Salvation Army held an open air service at 6 o'clock in the Market Place after the evening meeting and lot of people from all around would go. Well, of course, Uncle Billy was in the meeting hall and he followed the band up to the Market Place. One of the men from Worlingham spotted him and said, 'There's Billy Forman with the Salvation Army, that's why he wasn't in church tonight.' When he got home he sent a note to the Rector to say he'd seen Billy with the Salvation Army and that's why he wasn't in church. The Rector was so annoyed at this he wrote a note to Uncle saying, 'I understand you were with the Salvation Army instead of being at church tonight. Don't touch anything to do with my church until you make up your mind what you are doing.'

"Now he was bell ringer, he was church warden, he cut the grass and hoe the paths nearly every weekend all through the summer season and when a grave was required he was the one. Uncle was so upset he said, 'Well, if that is his attitude I will go to the Salvation Army,' and that's what he did. He had been so impressed with Sunshine's Memorial Service that he went forward with others at the end of the service determined to live as a Christian. I'm sure that if the Rector had had a word with him instead of sending that letter things would have been different. But Uncle Billy changed and things were certainly different for me after that, in the home, on the farm and in everyday life."

However the church was to have the final word as come Michaelmas they were given notice to quit the farm. One would hope that this wasn't a matter of vindictiveness on the part of the Rector but assume that the tenancy of the farm, Church Farm, depended on the farmer being a member of the Anglican Communion. So Michaelmas being the traditional time for farms to change hands, the family had to find somewhere else for themselves and their livestock. With little choice they moved to less than satisfactory land in the hope that somewhere better would become available in due course. And so the seeds were sown for the family to become committed Salvationists.

"Uncle started going regularly to the Army and to the week-night services. Tuesday night I think it was he got knocked off his bike. He got home and he got to bed and the next morning he called me. He called with such a kind voice

I wondered what it was all about. He asked me to go to the bedroom and see him. 'Cause he used to come bursting into my bedroom you know, shouting and swearing. So I went and he said, 'I can't get up Sam, I've had an accident, you'll have to do the milking and the milk round. You'll have to do the lot. If I can I'll get down and get into the cart so that I can show you where to go,' and that is what happened."

Even when he had recovered Uncle Billy decided to leave 13 year old Sam in charge of the milk round and being an agreeable boy he was popular with his customers, particularly with a Salvation Army family who always had a glass of lemonade ready for him. He soon became a regular visitor to this family's home and became very fond of their youngest daughter, Hilda. Following a memorial service for a young friend of his who had been lost at sea, Sam also transferred his allegiance away from the Anglican Church to the Salvation Army. Of course the milk round meant that he couldn't always get to the beginning of the meetings so he would leave his bicycle in the yard of these friends and get into the Hall in time for the band. On one particular occasion the rest of the family had already gone to the Hall except for Hilda's Mother who met Sam warmly, 'Hello Sam, nice morning, I hear that it's your birthday today.'

'Yes.'

'And how old are you?'

'Fourteen.'

'What did you say?'

'Fourteen.'

'You wouldn't have been allowed over my doorstep if I had known,' and slammed the door.

Sam bravely came back from the meeting with the other young people for a cup of tea. Only when they had all gone did Hilda's mother take her to task but Sam had never mentioned his age to her.

He had worked on the farm since the age of eight and was obviously old beyond his years. The family eventually relented and Sam moved on from that vividly remembered childhood, and what a hard one it had been, to working on his own farm by the age of 21 years.

"I'll tell you how it happened. As I told you, this farm was no good for us so Hilda's father said, 'We'll look round and find something to suit you.' There was this farm at Brampton, 60 odd acres, there were only a few acres of marshland down there. I was sent over there to be working until Michaelmas and he said to uncle, 'Now look' (because I had started going with his daughter you see), I would like Sam to be able to take the farm over when he's 21 yrs.' presuming that I was going to get married you see.

Uncle said, 'Oh yes, of course.'

"When the time came and I had started coming round to see Hilda one evening in a week, her dad said, 'Ask your uncle what he is doing about the farm, because you should be taking over at Michaelmas. Let me know what he says when you come again.'

"Of course I was keen to take over the farm. Uncle's reply was, 'If he want me out tell him he has got to give me notice properly.' I knew what this was you see. You get notice at Michaelmas and if you get notice to quit a farm you have to be compensated. So the compensation is you don't pay any rent for that twelve months. That gave uncle a whole year to find something and Henham estate let him have a nice farm."

Eventually Sam took possession of the farm as sole tenant. He was used to keeping pigs so his livestock comprised a few pigs and some cattle. The land was divided between pasture and some for hay; the rest was corn, mixed and root crops. Coping with everything on the farm himself with the occasional help of a horseman as well as keeping house proved too much and he moved into digs until in September 1931 he made Hilda his wife.

During those early years of being his own master he learnt a new skill which was to become a lifelong interest. "In a little cottage nearby there was an old chap keep bees, and he keeps them in the old fashioned bee skep, and when they swarm it needs another one, you can't control them. The skep is like a basket turned upside down, it's so closely woven because they don't want no light through. When you get a swarm you shake them off the branch or wherever they have settled into the empty skep. The old chap had a line of these and every time he had a swarm of course they came across my fields and he was so clumsy about it he just claimed the right to follow wherever they went and he'd walk through your crops and everything, very annoying. He never say, 'Do you mind' or 'I'll give you a jar of honey' or anything like that. So one day there was a swarm of bees and I thought I'm not going to tell that old rascal, I'm going after them. I got them in a cardboard box, got them home and hunted round for a beehive, and so I started beekeeping. I only knew from watching him but I did everything I could to find out more. Even when I lost the farm I brought my hives away with me."

The young couple were not afraid of hard work and the promise of their life on the farm was bright. All was well for two or three years and then the sequence of events is not entirely clear. Sam's in-laws retired and decided to move in with them in the farmhouse. Sam and Hilda had their first son; sadly it became clear that all was not well and the infant needed regular treatment at the hospital in the town. The in-laws did not take to country life and moved back to Beccles and Sam and Hilda listened to a bad luck story and took in a lodger. Then fate struck a hard blow and Sam lost the farm. Without consultation his father-in-law put the farm on the market, thinking that with her ailing baby his daughter would be better off living in the town. His motives were framed by concern but it was a cruel thing to do.

It was still a vivid and painful memory for Sam. "The farm went on the market 'For Sale with Possession'. Well you never sold farms like that, you have to allow twelve months from Michaelmas to Michaelmas to let that person in the farm to get somewhere else. I went over to the Henham Estate in search of a farm but they had nothing till Michaelmas. 'Course, I hoped and hoped. I was so sure that the farm would not get sold because farms were not selling. We had no idea that our lodger was negotiating for it."

Here was a young man who had left school at 13, had worked since he was 8 yrs. old, and had little or no experience of business or banks. He paid his rent when it was due but when the farm was up for sale it never occurred to him that he could approach the bank for a loan. The farm which had been bought for £1,000 in the 1920s was now sold for £600. If only he had understood the interest for a loan from the bank would have cost him less than his annual rent. As it was, Sam and his young wife found themselves both homeless and jobless. They had no choice but to move in with Hilda's parents. It must have been a bitter pill to swallow and as Sam reflected it could easily have broken their marriage. In one of life's little twists he was soon offered a job in a dairy. Things had moved on and milk was now being bottled but he still found himself with a barrow and a milk round only this time in a more affluent part of the town. It was 1936 when he came out of farming. Then war was declared in 1939 and Sam was called up in 1941 and a whole new world opened up for this country boy. Some people thought that as a Salvationist he would be a conscientious objector but he felt strongly that if you were called up you should be prepared to fight for your country.

Sam was suddenly in the army. Two months training; posted to be a batman/driver; Officer sick; sent on leave;

telegram 'Leave cancelled, return immediately'; put on charge for absence; Officer steps in; takes him to billet, 'Got your Khaki drill?'

'What's that.'

'Your overseas uniform.'

'I've only got what I'm standing up in.'

'Well, you've got to have Khaki drill, you're leaving here at 4.30 a.m. for overseas.'

Oh yes, Sam was in the army and everything happened so fast that it was all a bit of a shock!

"We were just Royal Army Service Corps troops and other men in the camp were Field Security Sections, and I'm with a Security Officer. We board a ship somewhere on the south west coast. We landed in Egypt and were sent to a camp outside Cairo."

At the outbreak of war, although Egypt remained a nominally independent country, the British effectively took control and it became an important military base in the Middle East. The British had a garrison at Alexandria, one in Cairo with a subsidary depot there, and it was to one of these in Cairo that Sam was sent. In June of the previous year the main logistics and training force for British and Allied Operations in the Middle East, called the Western Desert Force, had been set up. Nine months later the Italians invaded Egypt.

"Within three days we got our vehicles and everything we were short of and we started our journey from there to Bagdad, that's where the war was on. We got pulled into a camp at Jerusalem for a week, then when we left there we went onto somewhere miles north, sort of a little depot. There were some Foreign Legion, all horse riders, there; we used to see them go out, do a tour round and come back. Then I was taken ill, very ill. Captain said, 'Well, I'm sorry Private, you are not well enough to go on, we'll have to leave you here.'

"I said, 'Don't you do that, don't leave me here with that lot, they're blinkin' foreigners, they don't have nothing to do with us, won't look at you even, let alone speak to you.' If there had been a few British troops it would have been a different matter. I knew I couldn't drive, I was really ill, and of course you couldn't get any medical aid there."

The Captain relented, agreeing with Sam's request. "'Promise me that if I don't get through to Bagdad and you are still in the desert you will bury me properly.' I finished up in hospital when I got there. We were there exactly three months and the campaign finished so we came right back down to Cairo again by a different route when we were given seven days leave."

Whether it be in the midst of the blitz in London, following the British troops into Europe immediately after D-Day or in other war zones the distinctive Red Shield of the Salvation Army could be seen on the many canteens they set up for the Allied Forces. Their Red Shield canteens provided not just that all-important cup of tea but other basics such as chewing gum, toothpaste, soap and sewing kits and in some places they set up hostels and clubs for servicemen, and what a welcome sight they were to those men so far from home. A significant number of Salvationists died or were interned in prisoner of war camps but this did not deter them. Happily for Sam just as he arrived back in Cairo with some spare time on his hands the Salvation Army were setting up in the city. He was quick to introduce himself to the Officers and found himself staying with them for the remainder of his leave.

"And it was smashing. They looked after me, and people were going different places and I fitted in with that. In fact while I was there I went up and saw the Sphinx and the Pyramids, that was interesting. They kept in touch with me. And then after the war I got them over here for a weekend and they done the service in the hall. We had a lovely friendship."

Leave over, Sam's section was broken up and just he and one other, a sergeant, from those who had been to Iraq were despatched to a place along the North African coast. Conditions in the desert were not pleasant. In spring and summer days were unbearably hot and the nights very cold. The hot desert wind, the Sirocco, blew clouds of sand reducing visibility to a few yards, covering everything human and mechanical in grit and, as a driver, Sam had to keep the filters clear on his vehicle. Accomodated in a tent with the Sergeant-Major, each of them with just a blanket lying on the sand, when it came to the end of the day: "When I am ready to lay down and go to sleep I kneel down and say my prayers, and when I'd finished I said, 'Goodnight Sergeant-Major.'

'Goodnight. I don't know what you think you are doing talking to that tent, just wasting your time, wasting your breath, wasting your words and everything else.'

'I wasn't praying out loud. So I just said, 'I'm sorry you feel that way, but it won't change me.'

'You're wasting your time, a lot of nonsense, there's no one up there, and if there was what you are adoing, what you are saying won't go through the tent.'

I said, 'Well, alright. Goodnight.'"

They moved on as a section along the coast past El Alamein, yet to be the scene of so much bloodshed, on towards Tobruk. Camped some distance from the town, Sam was sent there with another soldier for company to pick up a rifle.

"We got into Tobruk, there were gates with guns each side. On the way there we could see smoke and hear guns from where the battle was going on; we were a bit chuffed because we were so sure our troops were pushing the Germans back. I went in and got my rifle, he stayed with the truck outside. I walked back to him and pointed to a row of buildings along the front. 'They look empty. I wouldn't be surprised if we're moving up here next. Shall we go and pick one out and tell the

Captain we've chosen a villa for him?' We started to walk and only got a few yards when I said, 'Tom, something is telling me to get out of here as quick as we can.' We got back into the truck and as we were driving out of the gate we noticed that there were men struggling with the guns and moving them round to different positions. Of course we could see right over there, it must have been two or three miles, the dust and smoke and hear the guns. You're in the war, it is an everyday occurrence. Just got onto the road and there were four little vehicles driving in. I recognised the driver of the second one; it was the brand new Salvation Army mobile canteen. I heard that they barely got in when the troops swarmed round them and then the Germans arrested them all, including the Salvation Army officer, and drove the truck away."

The siege of Tobruk which Sam brushed shoulders with would last for 241 days but for him there was more to come. They drove back to where they had left their section to find them all gone except for the Captain who had nearly given them up for lost. They were greeted with the news that Tobruk had been captured along with all the allied troops but the message had come through too late to stop Sam's trip. They loaded up the Captain's few things in the truck and made haste to get away.

"We kept going and going and at last we got to a place where we could get off the plain down to a lower level. That had been badly bombed and shelled, I was having a job going from one boulder to another. We picked up some more of the boys and then saw one of our other vehicles. There were two vehicles but you never park next to each other out in the desert because you make such a target. We stopped, I'm anxious to see who's there, bound to be three or four men. The Captain and I get out and there is the Sergeant-Major who had been driving one of the vehicles. 'Course the Captain is walking straight for him but the Sergeant-Major he come straight to me, throws his arms around me and said, 'I thought I was never going to see you again, I've been praying for you to come through.'

'Sergeant-Major,' I say,' did you say you've been praying?'

'Yes, I have.'

'But you told me you didn't believe in anything like that.'

'I didn't, but I've changed, I'm different now.'

Captain stood there and looked at him holding me in his arms. He went and spoke to him then."

By this time the light was beginning to fade and they thought it expedient to stop and brew their tea whilst it was still safe to make a fire which wouldn't be seen to give their position away. Many other retreating troops had gathered at this spot too and it was decided to make an early start in the morning. They moved on and their next stop was a place between a row of rocks where they felt it safe enough to spend the night…

"While we were sleeping that night the enemy had gone down the desert the other side of those rocks. We never heard a sound, nothing. When we got to the end of the rocks they cut to the sea and we're trapped in there. They held us for two or three days, all they could do was keep shelling. We saw them bring the guns into position. It was decided that we should go back to an opening in this line of rocks where we could get out into the desert. And we'd got to wait till evening, because of movement. When we got to this area where we had got to cut through, that's mined to the teeth. Fortunately there were four men with one little group that had got a mine detector, so their officer ordered them to go down ahead of us. I'm driving the first vehicle! [Sam gives a wry laugh]. There was one chap got impatient and wouldn't keep behind in line, an officer too, he drives past and of course was blown to pieces. He'd no business to overtake, you must keep behind the first vehicle, which we were most of the time. They cleared this pathway for us and we got through, and they keep clearing because they had mined acres and as they went they lay a white ribbon as it was cleared. Of course there is only room for one and I led the way, we drove all night. We used to carry a good supply of spare petrol and the Captain said, 'Let's pull up now before it gets any lighter. Fill up with petrol and send a message to the next vehicle.' You don't shout, you give a message to the next vehicle and they pass it on, there's a whole line of us. As it is getting a bit lighter you can see against the skyline the outline of big vehicles. They're tanks. The Captain told us to carry on filling up keeping as quiet as we could and he went to see who they were. We had hardly finished before he got back, 'God,' he said, 'it's the 25th Panza Division.' That's the crack killer tanks, guns. We'd just started to move and they let their guns go." Sam's voice broke as he relived this quite terrible moment: "They caught us broadside. We were the first to get away in the front, but they didn't move until we started to move and I suppose they saw that we were changing direction... oh, a nightmare. We eventually got to a place called Al Arish, there was the remains of a castle there, part of it was empty and we pulled in there to get under cover."

This must have been the castle built there during the Ottaman Empire in the 16th century, and one wonders how many conflicts it had witnessed during the next four hundred odd years.

"We were there a few days and I had to take the Captain down to base in Cairo. Eventually we fall in formation again and Field Marshall Montgomery he took over our part of the army then, so he was our Commander. We were fairly close to him. Then another war started, we kept going mile after mile. That was terrible."

Sam spoke no more of the North African Campaign; there were sights and conditions which he didn't wish to dwell on. However there was one occasion which he happily remembered. It was June 1943 and King George VI was flying in to visit the troops following the victory at El Alamein.

There was tight security on the road between the airfield and the camp, no civilians were allowed on the main road. Sam was not needed by his officer so he took a motorbike to go and patrol the route.

"I came across one man and I couldn't get any sense out of him so I gave him a lift back to the camp and he was locked up until the visit was over. Then I went back to the main road; the troops had got into the road by then waiting for the plane to land. I decide to go further along and they thought I was leading the party; this jolly officer called all his men up on both sides of the road standing at attention and I went flying through the middle and I just caught a glimpse of him looking to see who was following! Anyrate, I'm going along and I see this crowd coming down the hill towards the main road. So I stood my motor bike up and went to meet them before they got to the road. Spoke to them as best I could, we had learnt a bit of the language, they understood and were all excited as they wanted to see the King coming and I was hoping to persuade them to go back so that I could get back on the road in time. Instead of that away come these motor bikes, the outriders, and the jeep that he was in, he was in the back. And he could see that I was struggling to keep this crowd back, so I stood up and give him a salute and he turned round in the jeep and saluted me!" There was such a thrill of emotion in Sam's voice as he related this. "Made my day, made my day! I never forgot that."

Still with the 8th Army under Montgomery he was part of the second landing on the toe of Italy in September 1943.

"Yes, right on the toe. We gradually worked up yard by yard, foot by foot. Two and a half years I spent in Italy. That was a terrific experience because there were always times when you think you are never going to see home any more."

After four and a half years service overseas he eventually arrived back in England in one piece and was sent home on leave for what he thought was a month. Reporting back to the Officer at the depot he learnt that he had just three more months to serve before being demobbed so they thought they could find him a job in the depot for that time. However you would have thought that after nearly five years in the army Sam had learnt not to argue but the words just tumbled out, "Well, if you don't mind, Sir, I would think that after what I've been through I can have something better than that. I've never seen men having to lay in such filthy conditions in my life. I've been through something this four and a half years of war. I don't know how men stick it. I was brought up on a farm where they kept pigs, and they never allowed pigs to lay in the conditions that I laid in those nights and other men round me."

"Of course he got angry with me: 'If you can't take a job in this depot,' he said, 'you can go to Ireland.'

I say, 'I'll have to cross the sea again to get there.'

'Yes, of course you do.'

'I'm entitled to seven days leave before I cross the water again.'

'Alright, you'll get it!' came the gruff reply.

"As soon as I came back, hardly set foot in the place and we went across to Ireland, and do you know that was the best spell of my war service."

* * *

As with so many of the young men who came back from the war, Sam must have been a very different person. He had experienced things he could not have dreamt of when he left rural Suffolk and his young wife. There was no job waiting for him as the dairy had been sold to the Co-op and he was not wanted. It must have been a hard home-coming and no doubt it took a time to adapt. He never did return to his first love of farming but there was always work for him in the town, first with an Insurance Company and then life came full circle and he was selling milk again.

He was well liked and became a familiar figure when he was seen walking up the road on a Saturday in the summer with his wheelbarrow full of prize-winning chrysanthamums on his way to the Annual Horticultural Show. An even more significant memory would be of him in his Salvation Army uniform proudly leading the band back to the Hall on Sunday evenings with his two boys in the band following on. Life is full of twists and turn. Did Sam ever dwell on the thought that if he had carried on farming, which had been his dearest wish, then when war came along he would have been in a reserved occupation and would not have had to endure all the awfulness of desert warfare? Somehow I think not.

5
JACK

FROM HORSES TO HORSE POWER

"In a way I was part of a large family," Jack spoke reflectively, "yes, in a way. I've only one sister alive. I had another sister and brother, I must have been very young I hardly remember them, they got meningitis, it used to be fatal years ago. Of course, I lost my foot when I was about 6 yrs. old. When I was young we had a farm and my Father used to go into the barn on a Saturday and mix up food for the animals for the weekend so that all we had to do was go and take what was needed off the skip and feed the stock. Mother wanted a little rest so I went with him and played about. He was cutting the chaff with the chaff cutter and I thought it was an exciting piece of machinery so I climbed onto it and put my foot through the wheel... He didn't see that I was on it, he was busy cutting and he just cut my foot off, or nearly off. Then of course he carried me indoors, set me on the kitchen table and jumped on a bicycle or a horse and went for the doctor seven miles away in Attleborough. The doctor must have been there because he eventually rolled up in a Daimler or some old car and I was taken to the hospital, because my Mother didn't know anything about first aid, I mean people didn't in those days much — all she could do, I dimly remember her sitting on a chair beside the table and nipping my leg to stop the blood."

The doctor is likely to have come from 'The Pines' in Connaught Road, Attleborough, where the Medical Officer and Public Vaccinator and his deputy were based. At some time Jack must have been fitted with a false foot... "My Father wouldn't let me off in any way, he wouldn't let me shelter behind my foot. He encouraged me to do all the naughty things that children do, climb trees and ride a horse; and made me work on the farm and everything, which was quite good really, so it's been pretty helpful in later life. I haven't thought a thing about the foot. I haven't let the foot interfere in any way with my living," here he paused, "until recently; I can't help walking badly and that sort of thing." Born in 1901 Jack was now 94 and was finding the restrictions of old age and the old injury somewhat frustrating.

Both Jack's father and grandfather farmed a short distance from Attleborough, a small market town on the road from Thetford to Wymondham with a population of a little over 2,000. Although no great distance from the Brecklands this was an area of boulder clay, predominantly land for arable farming and not particularly picturesque. The town boasted a Corn Hall of white brick where the farmers from the surrounding area would gather on a Thursday, it being market day. It was known also for being the home of the factory and stores of William Gaymer & Son, the old-established cider producer and merchants, which was, no doubt, an important employer in the town.

"My grandfather farmed 700 acres. He wasn't really a good farmer, he didn't bother to cultivate the land, he used to grow a few oats, that was for his horses. He used to buy horses from the London Omnibus Company and bring these horses down in a batch – 7 or 8 or 10 of them – and he used to put them on the low meadow and get their feet right. They had been on hard cobbled stones so they'd got foot trouble. Then he would sell them to the farmers; mind you he used to make a good profit I suspect. Horse sales intrigued me. Spelman's was opposite The Bell in Norwich, towards Castle Meadow, they used to have a horse sale. [Spelman's was a long established auctioneers, chartered surveyors and land agents in Norwich and Great Yarmouth, but what Jack looked forward to particularly were their weekly horse sales.] I used to earn a bob or two taking horses to my Grandfather's farm. Sometimes I used to ride one and lead one; you had to ride on the wrong side of the road so that if anything came the horse you led could go up on the bank and couldn't kick up in the road. They used to trot the old horses out from Spelman's to the end of St. Stephen's Street and people who wanted to buy them used to stand and look and see if their feet were alright and that sort of thing. There used to be some old boys work at the auction to trot horses out. Gypsies used to turn up occasionally but they rather left it to the horse fairs once or twice a year; they used to be held on the Cattle Market in Norwich.

"Did I tell you about when I went to a horse sale in Covent Garden in London? I couldn't have been very old, went with my Father and my grandfather's youngest son, he'd started in the horse business as well. They took me with them and, of course, I was a bit of a nuisance and they noticed that there was a bit of a balcony, so they put me up there out of the way. What they didn't notice was a sack of peas or beans up there, and in those days all the old boys used to wear hard hats, top or half-way hats. So I looked over this balcony and saw them bobbing about in their hard hats and I picked a few beans and kept throwing them down and hitting their heads. In the end they kept looking up and my father saw what was happening and he came and squared me up. 'Don't do that; you'll upset the auctioneer!'

"My father used to rather like to buy calves; used to take them home and get them fat and sell them to the farmers. Sometimes he used to put them on the farms and the farmers used to feed them and then they would share the profit; he didn't want the bother of looking after too many. He had his customers you see. If they wanted a horse or a cow or something they would come to him and ask him to get one, rather than go to the auction and face the competition. He used to charge them so much extra on the top of what he paid for them – his commission.

"Going back to my grandfather, life in service has changed enormously. As I said, as a boy I used to take his horses from Spelman's horse sale to earn a bob before I started work and it used to astonish me that there were always several women in the house, two or three women in the kitchen. Then there was an old boy named Fred who used to take the horses to put on the mail cart; my grandfather used to supply the horses for the mail cart and they had to be changed at the pub when they had done a certain mileage. This old boy used to take them down and do general work on the farm. My grandfather also had a blacksmith and being a strict governor he hated people wasting a minute. Well, this old blacksmith used to do little jobs for my grandmother in the kitchen, anything that wanted doing and of course she used to make him a hot drink or a sandwich during the morning and she used to stand at the kitchen window and look out at the farmyard and she used to say, 'Walter! The governor's now coming.' And Walter used to shoot out." As he reminisced it was clear how different things were in so many walks of life. "If a woman had a baby in those days they would have a midwife in for about a month. My father, before he was married, used to have an old Welsh housekeeper. She used to wear black and when I was a boy she used to come and stay. Miss Barnard her name was. I used to think she was a witch.

"Father was very hard up for a time, it made him quite ill. As far as I remember the amount he owed the bank was a little over £100, £110, and he couldn't get that paid off. I don't suppose the bank worried too much about it, but he did, and he was so afraid they would foreclose on him. When I was a little boy I remember my grandfather used to come trotting round to ours in his pony and trap and he'd take a cabbage or something out of the back and say, 'Fred, I've brought you this, I thought your wife might like to cook this for your lunch.' He'd trot down there five or six times a week. Then the First World War came along and things got better; during the war he made a good profit and fairly quickly got the debt paid off and his health was ever so much better then. It really used to upset him, money. He brought me up in the same way really – if you can't afford it, don't have it."

Perhaps it was because of the memory of those hard times that Jack's father didn't encourage him to go into farming.

"I left school fairly young, 13 I was. I passed the Labour Exam to leave school. Anybody could pass it, it was very easy! The 1st World War had started and they were short of labour so if you passed the exam you could leave school, although I think it was mainly to put labour on the farms. My father, what he wanted was for me to be an auctioneer. He knew Salter & Simpson, the auctioneers in Attleborough. He knew Mr Salter quite well, he used to buy things in his Sale and he asked if I could be articled to him but the answer was, 'He can in time, but I haven't got a vacancy.' – whether this was an excuse I'll never know. Then my Father came along one day and said, 'There's a chap just started a garage in Attleborough and he wants a boy to serve the petrol and that sort of thing.' Well, of course, auto-cars in those days were a highly rated thing for boys. I jumped at the chance of going in a garage and I stayed there for 3 years as an apprentice. My father didn't have to pay a premium but I think I only got half-a-crown a week. The man that started this garage at Attleborough he didn't know very much about cars, he had been a chauffeur with an old car up in Yorkshire somewhere. Anyhow, he had this old Dietrich. I think the war [1914–18] must have been on because he sold it to the Thorpe War Hospital to take the wounded soldiers from Thorpe Station in Norwich to the hospital. He was like me, he just kept learning as we went along. He taught me some good things too, such as to get the heat from the soldering iron, instead of putting it near your hand you should put it near your face because your face is more sensitive, only he put it on a bit too far, not much, but I remember when I went home that night my mother wondered what had happened to my face and I told her and she said, 'Fancy that man doing that'.

"I remember my grandfather went to the Spelman's horse sale and bought me a motorcycle, which to my sorrow I never did get to go properly, I doubt if it ever would. He must have bought that after I was 14 and went to work in the motor business. I don't suppose he paid very much for it, he saw it there and bought it, thought it would do for the boy. It had a magneto on it and a chain drive which you would get your leg caught in if it ever did go. You remember the auto-wheel don't you? It was a little engine on a wheel, you used to attach that to the side of a cycle and turn it into a motorcycle.

"It was the only garage in Attleborough. There were very few cars on the road, but they broke down a lot. Every 5,000 miles they had to be decarbonised. No end of people with a squeak, they thought something serious was wrong. There was one old boy, name of Tripling, had a little two seater ARC, he was always in, nearly every night he would come in, 'There's a nasty little squeak in my car' – and we would fiddle about and try and find it. One old boy, I remember quite well, he had an Essex and he came in full of complaints about his car. His wife and daughter stood there and I said, 'You know you shouldn't be so fussy'. The daughter came to see me years later and said she would never forget that I was the only person to tell her Father that he was a fussy old man!"

Jack spoke of the different makes of cars which he dealt with in those early days – the Calthorpe which was made in Birmingham between 1909 and 1932 and sold from £175 up to £410, the Calcott made between 1913 and 1926 selling at £255, and of course the Buicks which were imported from Canada which could command up to £750 and the cheaper Essex from the U.S.A. with a starting price of just £195. No wonder he told his customer not to be so fussy!

"Cars then had detachable rims, Stepney Wheels; well that's another wheel with some clamps which you clipped over, you put it on the side. You didn't take the old wheel off and change it like you would normally do now, you would leave that wheel on and put the Stepney on the side of it and clamp it to the existing wheel – that used to stick out that much [gesturing] at the side." [The Stepney Wheel was invented by Thomas Morris Davies in 1904, a mechanic in Llanelli, as ready-to-use spare wheels for cars to carry. Over a hundred years later they were still to be in use in India.]

"In those days if you got to 30 m.p.h. you were doing quite well, that was really sort of a high speed, and I suppose they did 25 miles to the gallon. Some big cars with big engines never did so much, probably about 12 or 15. I seem to remember that petrol was 4 shillings a gallon.

"I had an uncle who had an interest in Mann Egerton in Norwich, he had some shares I think, and he knew some people there, and he thought I ought to go as an improver and turn into a first class mechanic. So he got me a job there and I had to go into digs, cycling home at weekends. I started at Mann Egerton's at 15 bob [75p] a week and I paid 15 bob a week for digs."

Now comes the first hint that although Jack always worked hard and long hours, he certainly liked to enjoy life too and always had a twinkle in his eye. "I always went to the Hippodrome once a week, I used to work overtime you see, and mess about there until 11 or 12 o'clock in case anyone broke down and then I would go out with the breakdown. I was only a boy really. The Hippodrome in St. Giles next door where the library used to be; it was a Music Hall, they didn't used to put on plays, they were at the Theatre Royal. I remember going there once with my Father, he wanted to go because a boy he went to school with used to box with a kangaroo on the stage and my father took me round the back to the stage door. Chorus girls used to be quite attractive!

"I remember I hadn't been at Mann Egerton very long and I'd never driven on the road much, I'd driven about the place and the yard. The work's manager, George Mainwaring his name was, he came to me because I was cheap labour you see. He said, 'I want you to go to Colchester,' or Chelmsford, I can't remember which it was. 'I want you to go and get Mr Mills' car, he left it there. It broke down and he left it at the garage there, and they've put it right and I want you to go and fetch it, he want it back in Norwich.' I sort of stuttered and said, 'Yes.' He said, 'Go to the office and get some money for your train fare and you can catch a train at Thorpe Station.'"

Over seventy years later the journey was still etched in Jack's mind. "It was summer time. When I got to the station I went to the first bookstall and bought a book on how to drive a motor car, Temple Press it was. I read that all the way. I found the garage and told them what I wanted and that sort of thing. I said, 'Do you mind putting the car going facing to Norwich?' The chap put it on the road you see. I don't suppose he realised that I didn't know much about it. I got in and came toward Norwich, I remember coming across the crossroads at Pulham St. Mary, I had always thought that was always sort of dangerous, my Father used to take me round there sometimes in a pony and trap, he always said that was a dangerous sort of place because cars were getting about, and I was very careful coming down there. Then I came past a customer's, a chap I used to know at Attleborough, a chap called Gatt. Jessie Gatt had left Attleborough and taken a farm near Pulham. I went past his house and I remember seeing that. I got back and as I drove into Mann Egerton's old George Mainwaring said, 'Thank God you're back, why didn't you tell me that you'd never driven a car on the road?' I said, 'Well you didn't ask me did you?' 'Well,' he said, 'you're back anyway.' Because as soon as I had gone you see, one of the mechanics who would have liked that job, and he went to old George and told him that I'd never driven, so George was, well you know, he nearly had a baby I think! He was pleased to see me back again.

"Next door to where I digged in Norwich the chap had three daughters and he was secretary to the town clerk in Norwich and he had a sort of connection, I suppose you could call it, with people who were getting interested in cars. I got talking to him one day and he said, 'I think it would be a good idea if I started a garage next door, how would you like to come and look after the car for me and start the garage?' I thought about it and thought it was a good idea. I must have been about twenty. Anyhow, that appealed to me and I took the job on. Then I found that what he really wanted was a driver, to drive a saloon car and take old ladies around Sheringham and Cromer, charging them for a taxi. I didn't like that, I wanted to start a garage, so I threatened to leave him. We had a talk and he let me put a sign up 'GARAGE'; that's how it all started. I couldn't afford a car then, I couldn't even afford a pint. I did used to buy cigarettes from the tobacco shop – May Blossom cigarettes and Matinée too. You could get Matinée in different flavours, American, Turkish and Egyptian, they'd got different coloured papers according to what they were, the American were white, the Egyptian and Turkish a dirty brown paper. And you used to buy Tennessee Wiffs, if you bought them by weight you got two more than if you bought them in a packet same price. I used to watch all those sort of things, 5d for five, or something like that.

"First car? I think it was an old bull-nosed Morris, but I had a motorbike before that. The girl had to sit on the pillion, then the wife came along and we had this basket sidecar – a real sporting model, streamlined! I put a hot water bottle in it when I took a girl out. We used to go and see my father and I had trouble starting one old bike so I got him to push me off, and he said, 'I've pushed this damn thing further than you've ridden it!'

"Anyway, I stayed and got married there and finished up there on £700 year, which wasn't bad because you know I only got £3 5/- [£3 25p] a week standard rate and the rest I used to make up on commission, selling cars and that sort of thing. Of course I had no working hours, I worked all the hours God sent really; I did work hard for him and his three daughters. People had driving lessons; I taught quite a lot of people to drive. There were very few cars on the road and everything was very slow and people used to get out of the way of motor cars; you did have to give way to horses, that law still exists. In the 1920s the early customers were quite well off I suppose, mostly solicitors and that type. Farmers bought cars, they were very convenient for them so they could get about to different auctions and that sort of thing, especially if he was a bit of a dealer or sold some stock.

"One man, Mr Sexton, saw a photograph of a car, the new Austin 126, and said he wanted one. I said that it was a new model and had only been out for a few days. He said, 'I like the look of it, I want one of them.'

'Well,' I said, 'wouldn't you like to try it first?' because I didn't like the design for an old man like that.

He said, 'You don't seem very keen to sell me a car, do you want me to go somewhere else to buy one?' So, I got him one, I hated the old thing, bad design but he said, 'That will do me.'

"It was a sort of sporting model, and I knew it was a terrible engine, noisy, not at all the sort of thing you would like to have. Anyhow, he had it about a fortnight and went to see his daughter who lived in Leamington Spa, he drove up to her house in this car which was painted an aluminium colour and she greeted him, 'Hello Dad, you've bought a tin car!' That upset him, he came back, 'My daughter doesn't like the car and it's noisy. I want you to alter that.' I told him it would take some doing and we messed around with it for two or three weeks without success.

"He came in one day and said, 'I've got a car coming down from Northampton, I want you to come and try it with me and see what you think.' A salesman had come with a nice Rolls Royce, a used one, nice car. So we went for a drive in it.

'Very nice car Mr Sexton, I really can't fault it at all,' I said. 'What's wrong with it?'

'I don't like the colour.' So without thinking what I was saying I said, 'Well, we'll paint it for you, whatever colour you like if you want it Mr Sexton.'

'I'm not going to have a second hand car that's painted, why can't you get me a new one?'

'Well, perhaps I can.' I happened to know that Mann Egerton's had one in their Bond Street showroom. So I went to see Pond who was the Sales bloke in Norwich and asked if he could get that car down from Bond Street so I can show it to a customer?

'I don't know,' he said, 'we don't run a Rolls Royce about all over the place; it costs a lot of money.'

'You get it down. If I don't sell it I'll pay your expenses for getting it here and for cleaning it up and getting it back to the showroom again.

Still hesitating he said, 'I'll have to see the Director about that.'

The Director's reply was more positive. 'You do some business with us, buy Austins and the like, so we will, on condition you pay if you don't sell.'

So of course I showed it to the old boy and he bought it on condition that I went on holiday with him, which I agreed."

From the very beginning of his working life Jack immersed himself in what were these new-fangled auto cars. He built up his knowledge and experience during the depression of the 1920s and during the Second World War when he was still in Norwich.

"Never really noticed the depression with the garage as those with cars had money and even in a depression some people made money. No end of firms went broke because they started making cars without really knowing how. The Austin company they were quite prosperous, they made a lot of good cars but they made one or two terrible ones which they took off the market very quickly, cars like the Hudson Essex. By the time the war started there were a lot more cars on the road, they were very popular and much more accessible, Ford made a car for about £110 in those days. The problems during the war were that you couldn't get parts, I used to keep people on the road with electrical troubles by fixing them in my own way, you wouldn't do that now, they just put in plastic parts which you can't repair; there are no skilled mechanics as there used to be. It was not unknown to spend three or four days scraping a set of bearings for the crank shaft; used to spend hours doing that sort of thing. Of course the oils have made a great deal of difference to the modern motorist, they have vastly improved as has the petrol – we didn't have pumps to start with, the petrol came in two gallon cans, it was Anglo-American Petrol.

"I used to have to go on night duty during the war. I remember when Norwich was blitzed we were on ambulance service and I was in charge of transport at Coleman Road, we had all sorts of vehicles that people had lent us. One of them was an old Bentley; if we had it now it would be worth an awful lot of money. Some of them wouldn't start, you had to swing them then. We used to pick people up from the bombed houses and take them to the rest centres. The Dereham Road was badly bombed, we found all the people in the pub's cellar. The daughter of the publican wanted to go to her bedroom before leaving, she had been a collector of Goss china, it was all smashed and she burst into tears. Another time we went after two old ladies and on the way one suddenly said, 'Oh! I've forgotten my hat.' Never mind that the Anderson shelter next to their house had been blown up. We went after another old boy in Norwich and he was filthy, hadn't had a bath in years, he was really a dirty colour!"

The war was over. Jack was still at the same garage in Norwich. "I was married and had two children and wanted an interest in the business. So I talked to two of the girls (daughters of the proprietor) and they wanted me to come into the business but the third girl didn't. We were friendly, you know, I was fond of them cause I used to mildly court all of them in the early days. Now they were all married. I could see that there was a family rift, so I told them that I would have to leave, and they didn't want me to – I'd been there since the beginning hadn't I? – but I said, 'Well I'm sorry but I must.' I was offered another job as a manager but I would have been in the same position as I was then, I had quite made up my mind to start on my own."

Then came the phone call that changed everything. 'How would you like to go to Loddon? We've made up our minds to sell the business there. If you want to buy it we'll sell it to you.'

"I said, 'I'd have to pawn my shirt.'

And he said, 'I'll help you as much as I can.'

"He was a fast talking salesman type, he could sell you anything."

Together they went to Barclays to try to raise the money; they had an appointment with two of the Directors. "Well, he tried to sell me to them, he frightened the life out of them actually. Strangely enough the Manager, not the Director, was a customer of mine, and he came round that night and said, 'I haven't got very good news for you. The Directors would like to see you on your own. Do you mind going on your own?'

'No,' I said. 'That's all right.'"

And it was. Jack was offered the money he needed and that is how he started out on his own in 1945.

"I'd built up a good repair business and everything, all sorts, so I spoke to my foreman, 'I expect you'll be promoted to manager when I leave.' However he replied, 'I shan't. I've got the same problem that you've got. I've got two children and I want to start a little business of my own. I shall have to leave as soon as I find a suitable place.' I thought things over and I said to him one day, 'You know what an awkward old devil I am and I know how awkward you are – why don't you come with me?' I took him on an equal partnership and that's how we started."

As it turned out the business took an unexpected turn. "When I first came over to Loddon I discovered one or two farm tractors in the garage here to repair, and I had brought one or two customers with nice cars with me, because over the years you build up a relationship. I realised you couldn't have tractors where you are repairing cars." Consequently Jack bought an old barn and launched the agricultural engineering side of his business.

It was in those relatively early years that Jack was approached by the Zenith Carburettor Representative with an idea to make a vaporiser in order to use TV oil in a petrol engine in tractors. They experimented and collaborated on the design until they were satisfied that they had produced something which worked. Then they needed to market it.

'How?' Jack's partner wanted to know.

'We're going to the Royal Show at York [the agricultural shows used to travel round the country then], I'm friendly with Whitlock the Tractor people. I'm sure that if I go to the Show I can get this vaporiser put on one of their tractors on the stand.'

"We went to see the chap on the stand, before the show started of course, and he said, 'You can't do that you can't have a tractor at the front of the stand, it's against the rules of the Show.'

'What about the old tractor you have pulling things about at the back?'

'Well,' he said, 'it's at the back of the stand, I don't see why not.'

"So we put it on that, but it wasn't long before we pushed that old tractor up front! We got two or three orders on that occasion. It was patented about 1950 and then, of course, to sell these vaporisers I would go round the country and look across the field and I'd say to the chap, 'Do you have trouble with this sort of thing?' and he'd say, 'Coo yes, I always have trouble to start.'

'Well, do you want to cure all that smoke?'

'What do you mean?'

'Well we make a vaporiser which would cure all that.' Sometimes it would come off, sometimes it didn't." A natural salesman, Jack found agents for his new product and a market in Denmark for them as the Danes got a rebate if they used TV oil.

Perhaps it was his grandfather's blood that ran in Jack's veins that made him such a good dealer, only now it was with cars and tractors instead of horses. He dealt with a lot of farmers and they used to deal, barter a bit.

"They nearly always used to deal, there wasn't a proper price for anything. There was an old fellow at S... Rectory, I used to sell him things, tractors and the like. I used to go and see him and he'd say, 'Come in and have a cup of tea,' and we'd have a chat and one thing and another, 'Oh, I don't know whether I really ought to buy anything,' trying to kid me that I wasn't going to make a sale; and then he'd go on and I knew exactly what was going to happen – 'How much is that old thing? I'm not going to pay a delivery charge.' That's how it used to go on. If I met him after I had retired he'd say, 'I wish you were back again. We used to have some good old times, I don't know if you made any money out of me or I made anything out of you but we had a good old talk didn't we?' Another customer of mine came in one day and said, 'I really need a tractor, but I can't afford it. I've got an old marsh I don't want particularly, if I sell that I could afford to buy a tractor. You don't want to buy it do you?'

"I asked how much he wanted for it, 'Well, I don't want it, but I expect I could let it to someone.'

'I expect you can, it's just coming when people want some extra grazing.'

'Well then I'll buy it.' I had it in part exchange for a tractor. A year or so later he came back to me, 'That old marsh I sold you, have you still got it?'

'I have. I let it out every year and get a little money back from it.'

'Well, I'll buy it back off you.'

'I nearly forget, I'll have to look up what I paid for it."

'I can find out, I know what you paid me.'

'Oh,' I said. 'Well you can have it for the same price.'

"All that sort of thing has gone out of modern day life hasn't it? Now they are trying to make the motor trade in the same manner, slaughtering the discounts that they are giving to the dealer so that he hasn't any margin for dealing. I had customers who came into me and never expected to pay what I told them in the first place, they always wanted 5% off or whatever I could afford to give them. I never played any fancy tricks with them, you had to try and keep your customers didn't you?"

Jack firmly believed that during those early years he had enjoyed the best of times in the motor trade. "There's no doubt about it. The motor car, amongst other things, has changed people's mode of living; it's made people more impatient, I'm sure it has, and aggressive. Because people who had a motor car, they thought they were better than the people who didn't have one, and the people who didn't have one were rather jealous I suppose of the people who did. And gradually now you can go up and down my street and see scores of cars outside nearly every house. I think the motor car has got a great attraction for young people, the age of 13 or 14, and after that the youth had got more sophisticated and the motor car is just another thing that has been here for ever. But the youngsters, younger than that can still appreciate a car that is different, like an old M.G. like mine, or a Morris Minor. I notice they look at my car as they go past. Modern cars look alike, even to me since I've been out of the trade, to a point I have to look at a car twice to see what make it is."

* * *

Jack led a full life, always with that twinkle in his eye. He drove his MG Magnette until he was 95 years old and died shortly before his 99th birthday.

6

THREE SUCH DIFFERENT LIVES

MAY – JOAN – SHEILA

No lives are ordinary, no two people the same but what are so different are changing times and circumstances. The lives of all three of these women were affected by war, two different wars; one could have been destroyed by the consequences, another found temporary freedom and fun whilst the other coped by taking it in her stride as best she could.

May was born in 1891. When I met her on her 103rd birthday she was sitting regally in the little front room of her council bungalow. Dressed in her traditional floral wrap-round overall, a jumper underneath, a cardigan on top, she received her visitors with enthusiasm. Bright eyes in her bewhiskered face showed her pleasure at all the attention she was receiving as friends and neighbours crowded in with gifts of gaudy brooches and necklaces which she loved, wearing every one so that you could barely see the colour of her cardigan. To mark the occasion the Mayor and Mayoress were there with a bouquet and the press photographer not far behind. It had become a regular event that on her birthday the Salvation Army Band would gather outside her home and play her favourite hymn 'Amazing Grace' and she would sing along. At 103, still in her own home, life was good, but it hadn't always been so.

She had married a soldier who had been in South Africa fighting the Boers. When the Second Boer War ended, May would only have been eleven years old. Did she remember her future husband as cutting a bit of a dash in his scarlet tunic, which would have been his off duty or walking out dress, although by that time the British army was fighting in khaki. Was he a boy soldier? In the First World War the youngest to enlist was 12 years old, sent home when they found him crying under fire and discovered his age. To young boys the far distant wars made glamorous and exciting dreams. Whatever the circumstances of May's marriage it was not to be a happy one as he turned out to be a very unpleasant man. Her repeated phrase was, "He was horrible. He was horrible." Presumably she thought she was marrying a nicer person but what had he been through in South Africa? The British won that war but at an enormous cost of lives. It was fought with the then modern rifles in a difficult terrain quite alien to British soldiers. In those days little was known of post traumatic stress; was his behaviour as a result of what he had been through, what he had witnessed or was he just an offensive character? So many questions but too long ago to be able to decipher his personality. Over eighty years later there has been no mellowing of May's feelings and she could still not say a good word about him. Both of her children had been born in the workhouse. This would have been the one at Shipmeadow; the Union Workhouse, the House of Industry or even called the Spike, chilling names for this bleak looking building. How would May have felt, young and heavily pregnant, as she turned in from the main road and came face to face with this two-storey H-shaped red brick building, the front over 200 feet wide, situated upon a slight rise at the end of a drive. All she would have seen as she approached was its frowning dark facade, no hint of the wings with the laundry, the bog house and what had been the pest house for those with infectious diseases. It had been built in 1766 to accommodate 350 inmates, the place the elderly dreaded, the place of last resort. This is the place May came to for care and a little comfort in the last days of her labour.

Life at home was not easy, her husband found work on Fridays as a drover at the cattle market but the money did not come to May, it was all spent on drink before the end of the day. When he did come home he would steal the food, meagre as it was, from the children's plates. Life was incredibly hard for May in those years but she managed and here she was at 103 the matriarch of the family with seven grandchildren and sixteen great-grandchildren and still singing along.

* * *

By contrast Joan, who was born in the middle of WWI, when she was in her early twenties, saw the advent of the Second World War as a huge opportunity to widen her horizons. Unlike May she had been fortunate in her education. An only daughter with one much younger brother, her Mother was a teacher and her Father ran an agricultural engineering business. She thoroughly enjoyed her schooldays and was a Girl Guide in the relatively early days of that movement, being a proud member of the Swallow Patrol. Her ambition was to be a hairdresser but she couldn't find a job and her Father's reaction was, 'It's no good your hanging about like this, you go off and learn shorthand and typing.' "So that's what I had to do. You did what you were told in those days and then I worked with my Father in the office."

It was when they were on a family holiday, the threat of war was brewing, that they heard on the wireless that they would like to bring women into the army.

"There were several of the local girls all joined up at Lowestoft Recruiting Office."

Joan made her bid for freedom and joined them. It was October 18th 1938 and Joan was twenty-two, strong-willed and capable.

"Oh, my Father was most upset and my Mother didn't want to lose my company." The decision to join up was taken amongst her friends and seen as an opportunity to get out of the Lowestoft area and do something different. The girls were in one of the first women's platoons. "That's why I've got the lowest number – W4, the 10th Suffolk Platoon. Colonel Chadd was our officer in command although he wasn't actually with us because, of course, we had to train with the men with the Regimental Sergeant Major. I had no regrets, learnt a lot, good and bad."

There had been just twenty-five women in the company in 1938; the number who enlisted increased ten fold over the following four years. Eventually over twenty thousand women joined the Service but that was a long way in the future.

"I didn't have a proper uniform for quite a while, they weren't ready for us at that stage." When the uniforms did arrive they were cumbersome and badly cut; they were issued with jackets with no cuffs, khaki skirts and khaki knickers with elastic bottoms. "There were several of we local girls all joined up at Lowestoft recruiting office. When the time came we all went off in an army truck [probably for their initial training at Canterbury] and the first night we had to sleep on sacks filled with straw, palliasses, on the floor in an old fisherman's hut." Although later they were billeted in private homes this must have been a huge shock to a young woman who had come from a comfortable sheltered home life but she seemed to take it as one huge adventure.

On 1st September 1939 Joan was called to the colours and early in the war found herself stationed at Landguard Point,

Felixstowe, supporting the anti- aircraft battery "ACAC 409 and searchlights. I think some of the girls took it in turn to go out on site or take over the telephone; others were cooks; they found out that I was secretarial minded so they put me in the main office."

As Joan rightly remembered, the first recruits were only offered the positions of cooks, orderlies, drivers or clerks but as soon as war broke out they took on many more rôles including radar operators, anti-aircraft-crew and military police. A.T.S. telephonists were sent to France in support of the British Expeditionary Force which was driven back to the coast and they were amongst the last to be evacuated from Dunkirk in 1940. By the end of the war the members of the A.T.S. had suffered a large number of casualties. However Joan did not have the opportunity of going abroad, probably much to the relief of her protective parents.

What she remembered was the later batch of recruits. "Then some London girls come down, they were terrible; I think they had been made to join up and they used to leave the iron on when they had been using it and do all sorts of bloomin' things!" The intolerant Suffolk soldier didn't have a lot of time for these 'furriners'!

Following her stint in Felixstowe Joan was posted to Hadleigh in Essex. March 1940 and Joan was made a corporal and shortly after that a sergeant.

"I think I had two stripes to start with, then they made me three stripes. When you were an N.C.O. like that it was a bit difficult because some of the girls were my friends and if you were an N.C.O. you weren't really supposed to mix with them."

On the whole she didn't travel far afield; the furthest north she was posted was Wakefield and then there were tours of duty in Harlow, Marham and Hoo in Kent. Despite her excitement at being away from home at last she had no wish to go abroad. "When the Germans started bombing over here we used to sleep with our helmets on. You just had to take pot luck whether you were in or out. It wasn't exactly a mug of tea or a bowl of strawberries!" By 1942 the uniforms were well cut and smart, the A.T.S. had openings for more than sixty different trades and Joan made recruiting broadcasts on the B.B.C. appealing to young women to join up.

"When the war was over we had to wait a little while and I think I had to go to Northampton before I was finally discharged. I was in the army for seven years. When I came back after being able to go here and there without questions asked I had to sort of start all over again and lead a proper family life."

Suddenly Joan's freedom was curtailed. Her brother, who was seven years younger, emigrated to New Zealand and Joan was left to work with and look after her parents for the rest of their lives, so often the lot of the daughter in those days. It could not have been easy but she accepted it yet always remembering those seven heady years during her twenties when she had found Army life so new and exciting. Joan lived to be ninety-eight and she was justifiably proud of being the oldest and longest serving member of the Auxiliary Territorial Service.

* * *

Born in 1919, in the shadow of the First World War, Sheila was the ninth of thirteen children – four boys, Jimmy, Jack, George and Reggie, and nine girls. The boys used to sleep downstairs. By the time she arrived on the scene her two older sisters had already gone away into service.

"Dollie and Fanny all went out to work first, then Elsie, Jessie and Edie. My Father was a Beccles man, there were nine in his family. He used to sell fish from a horse and cart, he would always come home about eight o'clock at night, we were all abed; he did have a long day. He used to like his beer though, well they all did, that was the way of life. I suppose when I was younger there were two horses, then they had three as two of my brothers had a horse and cart each. Jimmy and Jack went into the army. Father used to go down to the fish market at Lowestoft with his horse and cart and then he used to go to Norwich to get fruit. The roads were different then, I can remember going to Norwich once with him on the cart [18 miles] but I didn't like it, I don't think I went any more. That was a long trip."

Sheila's Father and brothers used to go with their horse and cart out into the country to sell their fish and fruit. In modern times it is easy to forget how difficult it was for those in the country to shop. Sometimes they were able to take the carrier into the nearest market town, country bus services were in their infancy and it was unlikely that in the 1920's they would have had their own car so they were often reliant on the pedlars and others who travelled around selling from their carts. When the fish man came there would be the inevitable herrings, cheap, plentiful and nutritious but also there would have been gurnards and weevers, the latter a coloured fish with a poisonous spine on its back. You could buy a whole basket of these little fish for sixpence [2 ½p]. They were sold with the cautionary warning, 'Not to eat the flesh off the head – it's poisonous.' Needless to say, the head was all bone!

The family lived in a semi in the town. "There was an opening into the back of our garden, the back yard like. There would be the dairy and the toilets, the sheds where the horses used to go and the wash house. The laundry was done in the copper in the wash house. My Mother used to bath us in there; she used to light the fire and we used to come out of that door to the back door and RUN!

"We all used to come home for Christmas. In time they had their own families and children, but we all got together and had a good time. The old Christmas tree was up in the corner. We didn't have a lot; I don't think we had a stocking, just a little present and that was the lot.

"I went to the Catholic school; we used to have to go to church you know. I don't know why we were sent there, we were not a Catholic family but we were all sent there; that is, until my youngest brother swore at the nuns. They come down and told my Mother that she would have to take him away but the girls could stay. So she said if you don't have the boy you can't have the girls. Then we all went to the council school down Peddar's Lane, the old school. I used to love school, especially playing games. We used to go down the common for our games; we used to march there from the school. Yes, I used to like lessons and different things. We never went to the High school 'cause we were just ordinary children and left school at 14 yrs. old

"I used to go up to my Auntie in St. Mary's Road a lot and help her. When I went home she used to stand outside hers on the opposite side until I got to the bottom of the road and wave and then I would turn the corner and run all the rest of the way home." There was a sale ground nearby.

"Fridays we used to make sure we got home before the cows come out. They used to pick 'em up from the sale ground and then drive 'em home didn't they; they didn't cart them anywhere. One day they'd got a bull with this lot and this woman went right acrost the track and he went for her. She went up in the air and down solid. I seed that, coo, yes, I got home quick. There were horses too; we never went to have a look, we weren't allowed. Plenty of old cows and that. They drove them out into the country, Bungay way.

"Tramps used to come round the doors. Auntie used to give them something to eat but she didn't encourage them. A number of them went to the workhouse which was along the Bungay Road at Shipmeadow. The little school used to be along there too, at Barsham; we used to go to the Christmas party because Uncle used to be Father Christmas there and they said 'Bring Sheila and Mrs W.'

"For our Sunday School outings we always went down to Lowestoft. In order to go you had to have so many Sundays that you bin to church. We used to go and play on the beach and were then taken somewhere for our tea before coming home. We never went back on the beach again. That was a treat in those days. Children had to make their own fun didn't they; they didn't get any if they didn't. Well there weren't no cars. I had some good times, Auntie used to take me on the bus to Lowestoft and on a boat on the river and my Uncle used to take me and my Auntie to the old cinema on a Saturday afternoon. All my brothers and sisters never went, my Mother never had the money for them but I used to go. Mrs Esling used to play the piano. Then I belonged to the Guides, I wasn't a leader but a seconder. If Peggy weren't there I used to take over and used to hate that. It was a good life, I enjoyed my younger days."

The time came for Sheila to leave school and instead of following her elder sisters into service or to work in the laundry she went as a live-in help to the aunt who had done so much for her in the earlier years. This aunt was considerably better off than Sheila's own family; she owned 'The Royal Oak' public house and a number of cottages. "I helped in the house but that was not the only job I had as I had to go and collect all their rents and I used to hate going to one of them because she was rude to me once but Auntie just said, 'Well, you are going to go.'" A fourteen year old grew up quickly in those days.

Then there was the day that Sheila met her future husband. "I used to bike over to see my sister [in Worlingham] and his mum and dad used to live opposite Dollie's bungalow and I suppose he followed me home because when I looked up he was beside me. He said 'Hello' and I said 'Hello' and that's how we met. He was working for the railway as a clerk, cycling to Haddiscoe, about an 18 mile round trip each day."

Whether or not Sheila and Peter would have had a longer courtship had world events not intervened we shall never know. In September 1939 when war broke out they realised that he would have to go into the army so they were married that year and moved in with Peter's parents. The following year Sheila lost a brother in the war and her new husband got his call-up papers.

"He was stationed all over the place but never went out of the country. He only had one night off, and if he got home on the Saturday he had to go back on the Sunday because he was on duty; he was in the Royal Signals. I used to go to see him in Nottingham, there was a nice person up there, Mrs Lambert, she was lovely."

The couple were fortunate as the railway continued to pay their employees. "I used to get money from the railway; his job was kept open for him for when he came back after the War. He was secure, he went straight back to the railway."

Next came what was probably the biggest change in Sheila's life; she was called-up to work at Elliott's, the munitions factory in the town. Until that time she had continued to work for her Auntie and had known nothing else.

"Auntie said, 'You needn't go, you can stop with me.'

'Well, I don't know,' I thought to myself, 'I would get more money at Elliott's and I am married now.' So, I never made no fuss and I went down to Elliott's. I was upstairs making the little caps that screwed into the machines. I loved it, I was there about two years until the time there was Cissy and me and we couldn't get these to go round, the screws wouldn't go right. So old George, our foreman, he said, 'You know what's the matter with you two buggers don't you?'

We said, 'No.'

He said, 'You're both pregnant.'

"And we didnt know, we just couldn't get the screw right; there was nothing wrong with the machine, it was us, we hadn't got the strength to push the thing down to go in."

He said, 'Get yourselves to the doctor and he'll tell you!' And of course, Cissy and I, we went and we were and we didn't know! I always laugh about that. Poor old George."

Without the outbreak of war it is unlikely that Sheila would have enjoyed the companionship of working in the factory, her first job away from family, which was a whole new world for her. Her husband came home safe and sound, he returned to work on the railways and they resumed their married life in the same town that they had been born in. Their family grew and when Auntie died they were able to move into her house, so that life for Sheila returned to the home which she spent so much time in as a child

7

PEGGY

...IN ANOTHER AGE AN ENGINEER...

P eggy – a pint sized woman with a positive attitude to life, always with a cheery word and always wearing a hat – we shall discover why...

At the age of ninety Peggy was as chirpy as ever but following a bout of ill health had moved into a residential home; ever appreciative of all that was done for her and she always had her Bible to hand. Throughout her life she was sustained by her faith. Again and again, whatever the topic, she comes back to the Church in one way or another. Peggy's upbringing was defined by the family's involvement with the Church. Her father was a sidesman at the big 15th century Parish Church and he taught the youth group on a Sunday afternoon in the nearby Mission Hall where their family worshipped.

"I was at Sunday School in the morning, Sunday School in the afternoon and Evening Prayer."

Back to the beginning – "I was born in Beccles on July 13th 1920. There were six of us. My mother lost a little girl of seven and a half with bronchial pneumonia. Today that wouldn't have happened and it was dreadful so I was told. They couldn't bear to even talk about it. My mother had Nell after that. She had three just under 3 yrs. old, Olive, Dorothy and Nell. They all used to be sent to Sunday School, all dressed alike. Then seven years in between and there was Alec, he became a submariner, then a couple of years Lesley, he was in the Merchant Navy, whom we lost, he was only 27 yrs. Lost him in '42. I've got his medals here in my handbag, posthumously awarded of course. Then there was me, the youngest."

The children had all attended the local elementary school and although they didn't go on to any further education they received a good grounding and Peggy was proud that the eldest, Olive, went on to become a magistrate. The only heating in the school was a small open fire, and maybe some warm pipes leading from the boiler, which meant that many, including poor Nell, suffered badly from chilblains. How many of us suffered from the painfully inflamed itchy red toes and worse still fingers until the luxury of warm schools and homes helped to keep chilblains at bay. Peggy was fortunate in not having to endure such discomfort. She enjoyed her school days even though she was aware that one or two of her teachers were 'a bit strange', realising in later life that they may well have been suffering from shell shock from the first war. A remembered achievement was being given a penny for correctly spelling the word 'phlegm'!

"There was no electricity when I was growing up; everyone had oil lamps. That's another memory of an oil lamp, I used to get croup as a baby, quite badly, and my Dad used to dip his finger in the bowl of the paraffin and just put it here (points at throat) and you breathe, old remedies, they worked."

Living conditions must have been a bit cramped when all six children were at home.

"When I was little, yes it must have been. Think Olive was born in 1908, I didn't come on the scene till much later because I had a cot in the bedroom with my parents. Well,

Olive married when I was eleven, and Alec he went. He started at the printing works, but he couldn't bear to be shut up. Now there's an irony, he chose to leave and go into submarines, well if a submarine isn't shut up! My dad was upset about that. He volunteered you see and he wanted to go into subs, and dad didn't want him to, and Alec said, 'If you don't sign my papers I'll get Mr Brindley up the road to do it.' He lived three doors off ours, he was a mayor one time and a J. P.. Alec got into the Navy. When he joined as a submariner he had to go to school at Greenwich and do the thing from basics; whereas he said that during the war it was a nightmare to have new recruits come in who didn't have the school training. He did seven years on surface craft, destroyers, and nine years in submarines, two years of those before the war. He was in the Kiel Canal the very morning that war was declared and they didn't know it; mind you it was expected."

In the latter half of the 19th century Clowes Printing Works merged with the Caxton Press in Beccles. It was only following the 2nd World War that the firm greatly increased the number of presses they operated so becoming one of the largest employers in the town and this is where Peggy's Father worked. Peggy was happy to reminisce yet her mind, even at ninety, was alert to the modern day and interested in the many changes there had been during her life.

"He was a printer's machine minder at Clowes. Clowes were at one time, I believe, bigger than Clays [printers in nearby Bungay]; but things rather deteriorated, Clays seems to be the better of the two now. Things would have been vastly different then, my Dad's machine would have been as big as a small room, whereas now things are so small. It's weird almost how things have altered. It's the same with photography, little tiny thing they use now. I think my father started life in Ringsfield [a village about 3 miles out of the town], but my mother was born in Beccles and my maternal grandmother was a Bungay lady. She had sixteen children, reared ten, 'cause in those days they lost a lot didn't they? Then she died at fifty-four and my grandad said, 'No one will ever replace my Agnes.' I've got her funeral card in here." [Once again Peggy delved into her handbag where all the special treasures were kept.] "I wouldn't have known her. My mother was the only one with her mother when she died, and I was the only one with my mother when she died, and she was twice the age I was at the time. She had me at thirty-nine, which I was then, and she died at seventy-eight."

At fourteen and a half Peggy's working life began, for the first year or so doing housework and looking after her employer's small boy. Then she began to want a little more money... "I went to work in a factory in Oulton Broad, the boss's name was Rist and it was the Beacon Lamp Company, they just made headlamps and side lamps for cars, and apart from the owner we had all foreigners. Of all things I used to spot-weld bi-focal elements for headlamps. I loved that, I used to sit with tweezers and pick up the filaments and vamp them between two copper rods, one comes down upon the other and you press your foot on a pedal and it fuses the joint between the filament and the foot, that's the stem inside the bulb."

This is 76 years later and undoubtedly she could have returned to her bench with enthusiasm and done the job just as well today but then motor manufacturing has moved on little.

When a girl of 21 left to get married Peggy's foreman wanted her to take over that position even though she was only 17 years old. "She had been on special works and I goes on that job and I made a good job of 1236's, the filament to be welded on one foot, one with the leg and go and be flashed with acid..." and without any hesitation her detailed job description continued. She did well and was promoted.

"Sadly it didn't last because the war came along and the whole firm evacuated. I would like to have gone, but my mum had Alec and Lesley away and I didn't think it was fair. So it was rumoured that Elliott and Garrood [marine engineering works] would possibly go into munitions, which of course they did but before that I worked at another place for Mr Rist; he had a cable works in Lowestoft opposite the Grand. At that time I used to bind the terminal ends, ends for aircraft and tanks, war work. I used to bind the ends, frazzled ends you know, with wax thread."

Once again Peggy launches into every detail of her job. Suffice to say that the end result was stout cables with lots of different coloured ends coming out.

Peggy left for work on the 7 o'clock train but long working hours were no impediment to her starting to court her Bobby; a courtship which was to last eight years before he became her husband. They enjoyed many walks and going to one of the two cinemas in the town. However Bobby was not a good time-keeper; he lived on the family farm a few miles from the town.

"The hours and hours I used to wait for Bobby to come in from the country. The whole family used to come in in dribs and drabs on their bicycles, and as they came in would say, 'He's now gone up to change,' or 'He's this or he's that.' Always late Bobby was. He's lucky to have me. We married at St. Michael's in 1946. If it had been a week sooner I'd have got some tax back. My sister Olive was good at dress-making and she did my dress, it had little covered buttons all the way down, she did all those. All my family could sew, my mother had three brothers who were tailors."

While Bobby was either working on the farm or driving for his uncle Peggy had started work in Beccles at Elliott & Garrood's...

"The war had just started when I went there. The first machine I was on had to have a cooling water, a mixture which flowed over certain types of tool, because some tools had to have a special tip annealed onto the end and friction is caused by the tool used for cutting so the cooling system was imperative really, otherwise that special tip would have fractured. They were making shells, 25 pounders. I had to come off that machine because I developed industrial dermatitis; I liked it and I was alright at it, but I had to come off it. I had to go in front of Mr Evans, the special referee for that sort of thing. He said, 'If Dr McClaren says you've got dermatitis, you've got dermatitis.'

"I went onto copper band then, that's a band of copper that is brazed into the shell where a groove has been cut, and tightened of course, and I had to rough the edge, take the edge off the outside and then shape it. I liked that too. My last job used circular saws, 18 inch and another one 22 inch. That was the job I was last doing, but right at the end when I left I was a paid supervisor, and I had done no end of different lathes, set for them and all like that, and even had an argument with one. That was in 1942, I was 21 yrs., that was in the May and I was 22 yrs. in July. I went to work one Tuesday afternoon and I didn't go home again for four and a half weeks. About five o'clock the girls drew my attention to something wrong and I inclined my head, thinking the machine had been stopped – a threading machine it moved slowly you see – and the teeth caught my hair. I didn't lose consciousness at all. There was blood lying around there for weeks with sawdust covered over it. Anyway a man picked me up, carted me off to the first aid room. Funnily enough a girl I went to school with, she put me on the bed, wrapped a clean towel round my head. Two minutes later the first aid woman came; we had two women, one on night shift and one on day shift, they used to go round distributing the cream you used to put on your hands before you started the dirty work, her name was Mrs Jones, she popped in the door, chin down to here. I said, 'Don't worry Jonesy, I'm alright,' and she talked about that for weeks.

"Dr Grantham Hill stitched me up in Beccles Hospital. My scalp got torn in five pieces and it had to be put – I only know what I was told of course – it had to be put on sterile glass, laid together like a jigsaw, before they knew where to put it back and I had a criss cross of stitches; they were purple, almost transparent, I think they called them silk worm gut or something. Anyhow they let that heal and all they did every day for a spell was take me down and shake sulphonamide powder on, it was quite a new powder at the time to combat germs and things, and that's all they did for a spell. Then, when they thought the time was right they wanted that taken off, and you'll never believe it, one day Sister Laws came to me and she said, 'Peggy, I'm coming after you in a little while and I'm going to take that off.' She did this in one of the hall-ways, sat me on a chair, came to me with a sterile teacloth, inside was a scalding hot piece of lint, she could hardly touch it, slapped it onto my head to coerce that skin off, I couldn't feel a thing. I'd been back at work for months before the feeling came back round the perimeter. She said, 'Peggy, you must be one of them dead end kids!' – they were all in the films at the time. Anyway, I got away with that one. In due time it came off, I keep going up and down and she would get pieces off as they would lift it and I could hear when she cut them with the scissors it was if she was cutting leather, until it all came off ready for skin grafting. I've got skin off my legs, two grafts, half of it took first time, and I had to go back again. I was in four and a half weeks, out four and a half weeks, back in three weeks, out a fortnight, back in a fortnight. Beccles Hospital, they did everything there then. But now, here's the rub, this was when they wanted to take off the first dressing of the first skin graft, that was this thigh [patting her thigh]. Sister said, 'I'll come after you in a little while, I'll put you in the bath.'

and she took me and put me in the bath, cut the bandage from top to bottom on the outer side. She said, 'I'll leave you twenty minutes in which time it should float away from you.' Float away! I think I'd be there now. Every patch was embedded. I got off the outside gauze, the bandage, and there was the padding, every patch you could see and I sat sweating and fuming, I kept trying to ease it off, I couldn't, thought to myself, 'What am I in for?' Anyhow she came back after that twenty minutes and said, 'We've got some trouble here. I'll give you another five minutes.' She did that three times and it still wouldn't come and there was I still trying and she said, 'Next time I come if it still hasn't come there is nothing for it I'll have to pull it off.' Back she came, she started here [pointing] and, she came diagonally across, and before she go half way I was sitting in blood. Shouldn't have been. 'Oh,' she said, 'can you put your weight on your elbow?' I didn't feel like that! and I had to take my weight on the sides of the bath and she had to let all the bloody water out from under me and flush me down. That was all because we had a new staff nurse that morning from Ipswich, it was a Wednesday morning, and what did she do, there on the side all ready was a tin of layers of Vaseline impregnated gauze, what she should have done was slap one of those on, which wouldn't have stuck; instead she put on Acryflavine, the yellow stuff they use for burns, the heat of my leg from the operation dried out everything and I couldn't sleep for three nights. That is the sort of thing that makes me bitter, because it shouldn't have been. I'll put up with kinds of suffering that you can't avoid, but that was avoidable. I didn't know about that until after, some people would have kicked up a fuss about that. I was in a state. Second skin graft went plain sailing. I've got skin on my head off my legs." So now we know why Peggy always wears a hat when she is out and about, because there is no hair on that part of her head, or as she so eloquently put it, "Nooo, I haven't got any hair on my legs!"

Although the early skin grafts were carried out around 3,000 years ago in India, the procedure as we know it today was refined and took great steps forward when treating those so badly burned during the 1914–18 war. It is amazing that Peggy was treated in a small cottage hospital in rural Suffolk but from her account the operation was still pretty basic compared to the wonders of the 21st century. However she survived and here she was at ninety describing it step by step.

"One Sunday in hospital I had fourteen round my bed. I wasn't ill you see. They sent me to have a photograph taken with some of my girls, the others would have been on night shift." [Once again she delves into her handbag; what a treasure trove it is.] "My head all done up, bandages under that square I've got on my head. No pain, the nerve was severed you see, but I'll tell you what I did feel, I was away from work for nineteen weeks and things had gone a bit haywire whilst I was away because there was a contract I was in charge of. There was a big box of rejects and the first thing I did when I went back, I got two of my girls to sit and chalk on after gauging where the faults were and quite a lot of them were threads so I put myself on the machine – the very machine I had the accident with – and picked up a lot of the threads, put them through and they went alright; but it was so time-consuming keeping me away from what I wanted to do for the rest of the job that I trained one of my best girls to do that. I don't know what went on while I was away and I did think to myself, 'What a thing to come back to.' But I did notice apropos my head, there was no feeling on the top. If I wanted to take the oil from the sump and re-oil it, a certain amount of swarf would gather in the bottom you know, small shavings, and if I had my head down, when the feeling first came back it came like a perimeter, like a gas jet, it would feel hot, until it gradually became as though it was normal. And if I used to ride on my husband's motor bike, pillion at that time, I sometimes had to get him to stop, because the feeling in my head wouldn't be quite as I wanted it, and then it would recover. But it all worked itself out, and I'm still here to torment you! My biggest worry was that it was a hard year for my parents. I got back to work and in the November we had the news about Lesley. I'd been back to work about a fortnight and I think his ship was lost on 1st November. He had been on the Anchises and other ships in the Blue Funnel Line… the merchant navy, they used to call them the scum of the sea, but they held our shipping lanes open, and they had one little gun on board. I can't imagine whether it was safer to be in convoy or just ordinarily going along, because if you were in convoy weren't you more of a target? The strange thing is he went to sea on that boat with another Beccles chap, they were both allocated to separate lifeboats. The other chap got in and he's still alive in Beccles, but he never come round to ours any more, he couldn't face it."

During the 39–45 war The Blue Funnel Line alone lost 41 ships and 324 lives.

When that contract was completed it seems that Peggy moved on to another job… "They were mortar bombs, solid steel. Eight to eight and half past four on Saturdays, they had hardly any time to shop. My work began when the other girls left off, yes, tool-setting. During the day things are going along swimmingly unless you have a bit of trouble. I did have a machine that I had to grind two different size drills for, one inch and nine sixteenth and one inch and three sixteenths. Well you had to drill, one goes down further than the other and they were solid steel billets, and if one caught a crab as we called it, some piece of steel that fractured the drill, I had one fracture one day, about an inch and a half back, and I had to go into another department on a rough grinding wheel and grind all that back, all that steel, before I could pick up that shape again on another machine. The sparks flew, they spoilt my glasses, they don't give you goggles to wear. I hadn't been there long before I was told that one of the men was told to keep an eye on me, in other words, bring me out. The girls thought I was going to be their foreman, this was before I was on another contract, and they found that it didn't work out like that, somebody else was made foreman, but that didn't worry me. I wasn't upset, I said I wasn't cut out for office work, I'd rather be with my hands. I've liked whatever I've done and sometimes I lie in bed at night and think, 'I wonder if I could do that now?' My hands aren't up to it. Nothing's the same today. I often think I would like to see how things are done now. When I gave my notice in, Mr Garrood he came three times and asked me to stay on and I said, 'No, you're getting rid of single women and keeping married women and I don't agree with that. I was shop steward at the time."

So Peggy started her life as a house wife and then a mother. Out in the country where she was now living she had to adapt to the lack of utilities that she had become accustomed to in the town.

In the '20s they didn't have an inside bathroom or toilet, or as she so graphically put it "Who did? Even royalty way back had earth closets." She went from flush toilets in Beccles back to basics.

"When I first married, would you believe, water didn't come to Shipmeadow" [a village between the two market towns of Beccles and Bungay] "and I had to take buckets down to the pump, it was in a piece of someone's garden down the bottom. I had to take half a bucket of water to prime the pump. So each time you took two buckets back you still only had a bucket and a half."

She was as practical as she had been brought up to be... "I used to go to Gunn & Hill's [the ironmonger's], I went in there once and I said to the chap, 'I want a shoemaker's knife please.'

He laughed, 'What do you want a shoemaker's knife for?'

'I want to mend my girls' shoes, my dad always mended ours.'

"I always liked doing things like that, electrics and that. I still got a spare element for an electric iron. I use an ordinary iron, I've got a steam one, I've got a heat-controlled one, but I don't use them. I wanted a new one, I wanted an ordinary iron that I could maintain myself, because Bobby and I always did our own repairs; and I got an ordinary iron from the electric light shop, due for export only, and I've still got it and I've still got an element I can put in it. I've always done that sort of thing. Before I married I used to put washers on taps at Frederick's Road, four houses went to one water cock and I used to get on the pavement and use the proper handle. I used to go to four houses, first ours and three others and ask them would they take some water until I'd put a new tap washer on. I just did it, I'd got brothers at sea, dad often on overtime, I just used to do that sort of thing. Sadly, my hands are such that I can't twizzle a screwdriver like I used to or hold the screws."

Just imagine if Peggy had been born into the age of of technical colleges after the war what sort of career she may have pursued?

8
DEAR BETTY
DAUGHTER - SISTER - WIFE -MOTHER

To Betty family is all and over her life she has cared for her brothers, father, two aunts and parents-in-law and latterly her husband during his long final illness. She is always cheerful and has a ready laugh. Her household chores are done long before most of us are awake, her home spotless, the grass on her lawn is polished! Betty is always neat and trim and when you bump into her in the town you always come away feeling the better for it.

Her memories are vivid and the words tumble out...
    "I was born June 25th 1930. I went to school and at thirteen I left to be housekeeper to my dad as my mum died at the early age of thirty-five in childbirth. We had a housekeeper for two years because I was only ten when she died and then when I got thirteen I took over for ten years until I got married. My brothers were 7, 12 and 14 and dad was forty-one, left with four children. 'Cause there wasn't any help then but we did have one Red Cross parcel from the Area School. That was the only help dad ever had and he was only labouring at the time and earning about £4 10 shillings a week. He used to walk to Darsham to work [15½ miles] and ride home on the

lorry. He was a really good walker. He was one of the best, we couldn't have had a better father, well he was like mother and father to us all the while, he really looked after us. He appreciated what I done because if the boys got fighting or anything, which they did, amongst theirselves, his work mates used to say, 'Well, how do you correct the boys?' he used to say, 'I don't do that, Betty do that.' They were good lads, they worked hard, they had paper rounds. Jim went fishing when he first got married, he even went on the boat at Lowestoft and he couldn't swim; he went on the trawler, stuck it out for the money. He had a hard start but he got through it. They've now been married nearly sixty-four years, they were only 19 and 20, so you see through hard work it is surprising what you can do. Everybody said it wouldn't last but it did you see – working together, and he went as a Bevin Boy. The other two did the voluntary two year service which was in at the time [National Service] which made them. I mean they were no trouble, they never got into trouble and they worked hard, and dad was proud of us all, we never brought no trouble home. We respected him."

When the family moved in the 1920's to a two up two down terraced house quite near the town centre they had just two boys: it was in this house that Betty and her younger brother Charles were born. Then the first houses of what was to be a large council estate were built and they were fortunate enough to be given one of these...

"Then we moved up to Castle Hill. We were the first ones to move up when they were built. 7s 6d [37½p] a week, that was quite a lot in them days; we did have electric and everything on up there then and we loved it. That was a three bedroom house. We had a happy childhood, it was hard ... I remember my mother, I remember her well, she did die in childbirth, that was still born. Anyway that Monday morning, 'cause that was wash day, all day then weren't it, and ironing on a Monday, and they had the boiler to boil up and that; the copper was in the bathroom. You had the bath and then you had the copper beside it, because you could heat your hot water and put it in the bath you see. That morning when I went to school I said, 'Is there any shopping you want done Mum, a loaf of bread or anything when I come out of school?'

'No, I'm alright for that,' she said, and that was that.

"She died, no she didn't die, she collapsed at three o'clock in the afternoon. She was baking the tea for us, 'cause there wasn't no school meals then, and she was baking and she come over with the heat and fell and knocked her head on the oven door. The neighbour next door, she could smell burning and she come round and found my mother in a pool of blood. Of course she got the ambulance and just as I was coming up Castle Hill with my friends out of school I could see a lot of people round my gate and there were two police people there, and I went to go in and they held me back. 'You can't go in for a minute, go with the neighbour.'

"I just saw her head on the stretcher as they took her out. So, I went with one of the neighbours and I didn't learn till afterwards that they took her to the hospital and she died about 4 o'clock. She lasted about half an hour when she got to the hospital. The doctor say today that if it had been now she would have been saved, but they couldn't do it then she had lost so much blood. 'Course poor old dad he was at Darsham and he come home – what a dreadful shock. I learnt a lot more as I got older. Poor lad, they got him home and it was all over, she'd gone. Yes, he had a terrible shock and at 41 left with four children. So, that's how that happened .

"She was a lovely mum so kind. Didn't go to work, mothers didn't so much in those days, she was always there when we came out of school. Most people didn't have a lot of money but we had a lot of love, a happy life. We were a family. At Christmas we had a stocking, we used to have a bit of coal in it, for luck, then we had to empty it onto the fire and the stocking shrunk! Then we had one of them little balls of elastic, like we used to have on the fair years and years ago, and an orange and an apple and nuts, that was about it. Then after dinner we used to play ludo and the gramophone, His Master's Voice, we were allowed to go in the front room and have a game of ludo an' that. Oh yes that was our treat to go in the front room at Christmas. During the afternoon after you'd had your dinner, which was rabbit mostly or a bit of beef, then jelly and fruit, then we could eat our orange. Me being the only girl with the boys, they didn't really want me to go on the common with them, 'We don't want girls with us!' One Christmas our dad made a sledge and said, 'You can go on the common with them.' Outside the golf house there used to be a slope and with the snow you could slide down there. Mind you there was water at the bottom – on the green it was frozen. So they said, 'Oh you can come and you can go first and then you can go home.' Well they pushed me so hard I went in the water. I went home upset and dad said, 'Whatever's happened?' So when the boys come home he smacked the hands on all three of them and said, 'Well I'll have the right one I think.' He was comical. So I didn't want to go no more."

Despite life without a mother and the responsibilities that Betty had to shoulder at such a young age the family managed to enjoy themselves.

"Then the boys wanted to go to the Saturday matinées up the Regal. So we used to all go down to Barsham and do some fruit picking, blackcurrants, at eight in the morning and earn enough money to come back, go in the toilet in the Old Market to have a wash and go down to Mr Fitt's and we used to have our chips and peas and then we had 3d [about 1½p] to go to the cinema, the Regal, in the afternoon. Sometimes we sat in there twice and see it through again. Then we went home. What a day! That was beautiful. The Fitts, they were a lovely family; because I couldn't buy no clothes with the clothing coupons, Mr Fitt he used to say, 'I'll buy your coupons off you Betty for the girls' and then I used to get black market sugar and tea and cheese for the lads you see, to survive, because they took some feeding, four of them with dad. You see there were a lot, they had good appetites, in fact, my brother Dennis, he was the one, as soon as he got home he'd charge into the pantry and so in the finish dad put a lock on because he used to eat nearly all the bread. Yes, bread and cheese, he always had a big appetite, he was a devil. Well, anyway we fooled him, he couldn't get in. Beautiful memories."

It was quite a juggling act for Betty to make ends meet but she and the boys were never lacking in initiative!

"When I was looking after them I thought I must earn a little bit of pin money, it mustn't be all housework and cooking, which I done. I mean I made them beef puddings and steam puddings. They lived well with stews and whatever and rice puddings. Then one week, I don't know if I should mention this, the two boys had a belly ache, they hadn't been to the toilet. I think to myself 'Now what do I do?' so I got some Epsom Salts and I made a rice pudding and I put a tablespoonful in, that sorted them out. They said, 'Oh, we've been Betty, we've been,' and I said, 'Thank goodness for that.' My dad laughed about that, he did. After that every week they had a teaspoonful in the rice and we had no more problems. No, they didn't know nothing about it! Then our dad, 'cause we all had curly hair and Charlie was a blonde, full of curls, and he was about eight, so dad left 7d and said, 'Get his hair cut.' I looked at that 7d and thought I don't know I could get some stewing meat for that because it was cheap in them days. So I put a basin on his head and cut round it. He looked like a little monk. Well, he came home from school and said, 'They laughed at me.'

When dad come home from work he said, 'Whatever's happened to the lad's hair?'

I said, 'Well I saved 7d.'

He said, 'You can't do that, you take him up tomorrow and get that shaped properly, as a boy.'

Charlie laugh about that now. One day he had a hole in his trouser pocket, his shorts, because they didn't go into long-uns until they were 14 yrs. in those days.

'Alright, keep your trousers on', 'cause he was ready to go to school, I said, 'I'll soon sew that.' When he came home from school he said, 'The teacher had to sort that pocket out Betty because you sew it to my pants and I couldn't get changed to put my shorts on for games.'"

When Betty left school at just thirteen her headmaster, a much loved and respected man in the town, had put his arm round her shoulders and described her as the youngest housekeeper he had ever seen. Yet she coped with the common ailments of coughs, colds and ear-ache as well as the cooking, washing and general housekeeping. Understanding how times have changed today she felt that she would not have been allowed such responsibilities and wonders if the family would have been broken up. In fact, at the time of her mother's death one of her mother's sisters had offered to adopt Betty and give her a good start in life. Her father put his foot down and refused to allow the family to be separated and so they worked as a unit with Betty, the only girl, very much in charge.

For entertainment at home they had a battery-powered wireless which their father listened to for the news and the football. If the battery ran low during the football one of them [they took it in turns] was despatched to run as fast as possible to 'Morlings' in the town where the battery would be charged for 6d [2½p]. There was a wind-up His Master's Voice gramophone, originally with wooden needles, or they were just content to read, with the library being a popular port of call. As she got older Betty was allowed a copy of *People's Friend*, a magazine still published to this day, and the boys had their comics, *Beano* and *The Dandy*, which, once read, would be exchanged for different ones with other boys living in the road.

Dennis had a paper-round and at a farm where he delivered he was encouraged to pick up the windfalls and take them home to Betty so that she could then make apple pies. Today that farm is long gone and has been replaced by one large housing estate. There was also an apple tree in Banham Road, an area still with only a few houses before it too became consumed by concrete, and Dennis, delighted with the first lot of apples which he brought home, says to younger Charlie, 'I'm going up there to get a few more apples for Betty, keep on guard.'

Betty takes up the story, "So, of course he got up the tree, don't he, and opposite, about two doors down there was a policeman live there with his wife. He come out on his bike, 'cause they had bikes in those days, he said, 'Hello Charlie, what are you doing?'

'I'm just waiting for my brother.'

'Well, where is he?'

He looked up and said, 'Up there.'

'Come on my lad, be careful and get down that tree. We won't take no notice of that, but don't climb up there because you'll be falling and hurt yourself.'

Dennis said to Charlie, 'Why did you tell him where I was, you look straight up!'

"That cop did laugh. The policemen were friendly in those days, you could talk to them; they knew the youngsters and the youngsters didn't abuse them like they do today."

Betty's maternal grandparents lived in nearby Bungay. "Grandad was a tailor, he made my Mother's wedding suit. After mum died Charlie and I used to go over on the bus to spend the weekend with them sometimes and holidays when we were right young. On a Sunday we weren't allowed to run. That was church in the morning and my aunts were in the choir at St. Mary's and then we'd come home and change and sit and talk and whatever. When Nanna was getting the dinner ready I used to help even then. Sunday afternoons we went for a walk then in the evening we went to church again. She was strict but she was lovely. They lived a big age, grandad was 92 and nanna 91, they stayed in Bungay all that while. Grandad was still a paperboy at 83! He thought, 'Well, I can't just sit doing nothing,' and when the newsagent said, 'Do you want a job, William?' he said, 'Have the bag ready and I'll come and get them.' He done it two or three years. He loved company he did."

Her father came from a Beccles family. As a young man he had enlisted and was sent overseas during the First World War. Betty wasn't sure where he had served but she did know that he was pretty ill when he was gassed. By the 1920s he was happily married, a hard-working man doing his best to support his wife and growing family. Together with his war time experiences and then being tragically widowed at such a young age with four children to care for he must have felt that life was conspiring against him. By all accounts he was a quiet placid man but perhaps his hard life accounted for his love of walking as a means of relaxation. He died in his sleep at the comparatively young age of sixty eight.

"Dad always used to go for a stroll on a Sunday, he used to have that for his day, to get away and relax. He never remarried, there were several women that wanted to marry him but no he kept himself to himself. He wrapped hisself round us. His stroll, he used to leave a note Sunday mornings when he got up because he would leave about half past six, summer time of course. 'Just going for my stroll, see you later, behave yourselves. Betty I'll leave you to keep an eye on the boys.' Anyway off he would go, he used to walk from here to Lowestoft [about 10½ miles], Lowestoft to Yarmouth [about 11 miles] and back again, all on a Sunday. You see he was six foot and took long strides, that's why we runned beside him. That's why I walk quick!" [And as Betty appoaches her nineties she is still running, a five foot nothing bundle of energy!] "We all walk quick, can you wonder at it. He was a marvellous man for walking. He'd worked hard all week and do you know there weren't a blemish on his feet; when he died in his sleep even the doctor remarked, 'I've never seen a man with feet like it.' He never had a corn, nothing. Hob-nailed boots for work but he had his punters, they were a plimsoll sort of thing, for walking. Once he took one of his old army friends, who he knew when he was in the First World War. 'Next time, Jim, when you want to go on one of your strolls just leave me at home, don't ask me.' He'd got blisters and I don't know what!"

Although the family made their own fun they also found it elsewhere! "Sunday evenings dad used to take us for walks and he made sure that we went to Sunday school. When I found there was going to be a Sunday treat, 6d on the coach, I used to join that church. We went from Salvation Army to the Methodist; you name it and we went where the treats were. One outing we went to Lowestoft with the Methodists, on a bus, and we all went on the beach, and then we went in at tea time and had our tea, a couple of cakes, jelly and fruit, and then they'd bring us home again. So we had an outing you see. If he won a penny at alleys, Charles used to run down the Co-op and get a penn'orth of shelled walnuts and we used to share them between us. That was luxury now and again, 'cause he could win at 'em. Sunday afternoons they used to play outside, either a game of football or fivestones."

Betty used to be getting their tea ready, she opened a tin of pineapple, there was a pile of bread and butter, celery and she made some coconut buns. "One of them would say, 'I'm just going in,' and then another went in. I'd say, 'Right we'll have our tea now,' and in we'd go and all they had in their dishes was juice, they'd been going in taking their three chunks of pineapple. I said, 'I've got mine here look and I shall enjoy it, you'll have to have your bread and butter and soak it in your juice.'"

For other treats, "There was Ellwood's sweet shop. Mrs E. was a straight-laced lady, she used to have a high collar. She was a big woman, always wore black, she used to frighten me to death. I only had enough to get two ounces and I had to make my mind up before I went in the shop, otherwise she'd say, 'What do you want?' very gruffly, she was fierce. So you had to be alert.

'I'll have some jelly babies please.'

'How many?'

'I've got threepence.' That went a long way then.

"I can see her now and she always had this lovely gold watch, and she had fat wrists and that watch sort of dug in her wrist and do you know that fascinated me. You know a child; I thought that won't be very long before she can't see that if she gets much fatter."

Despite having the home to run and looking after the family, money was short so it was not long before Betty took her first of a variety of jobs. First, when she was only 12, she took a Saturday job cleaning for an ex-Mayor of the town and his wife.

"I always remember that there was always a half-a-crown left on the sideboard and every Saturday that I went there it was still there. She was trying me out. When I told my Dad he said, 'Well you're going this morning, when you go up there tell her, thank her very much but you won't be going no more.' He could have gone up there and blow up but he didn't want any of that, but she knew what he meant didn't she? What a nasty thing to do. Terrible to leave a half a crown like that to test a 12 year old.

"When I was about 13 I was a waitress at the Tower Café for Mr & Mrs Judge. They were kind to me. When I came out of school I used to go in my black tunic and black stockings for about an hour three times a week and Saturday morning. They had a guest house next door so on Sunday I used to go at nine in the morning and go and clean the shoes. I used to clean the shoes and put them outside the doors, I had a number to know which ones to leave out, then lay the breakfast table, set that all out and then go through to the kitchen and mix the Yorkshire up ready for the puddins. Then there was a little brush and dustpan, I didn't know what that was, I thought it was a bit little to sweep the floor. 'That's for the table crumbs, Betty.' So I learnt something else!

"Then dad said, 'I've got you another job, Bet.' Friday nights I used to go down to Elliot and Garrood's and get their order for fish and chips.'"

Elliott and Garrood's was a well established engineering firm in the town who specialised in making marine engines and allied equipment such as winches and line haulers. That is until war broke out and for the duration production had to adapt to munitions and other war work. This is when Betty would have been popping in to get their weekly supper order, "Twenty four orders, one and one, fish and chips. I used to get six shillings for that. Then Mr Fitt asked if I could go half an hour earlier as I was holding everyone up! I asked him to salt and vinegar them all before he wrapped them, then dad said one of them didn't like vinegar and I said, 'Hard luck then I can't tell them to leave one out.' I done that for several months. I used to run up there and back to Elliots' with it and then back home again [one end of the town to the other]. I've been running all my life, good job I've got a good pair of legs and feet!" It was at this time that a bomb dropped on a house in the town, "My friend , who I went to school with, her Mother got killed in their house, it was a write-off. Her husband was fighting in the Air Force and Elizabeth, she had gone to a Guide meeting or something, so Mum was in there alone. Yes there was a fair bit of damage, but I can't remember nothing too heavy. Norwich and all around took it bad, we could hear them coming over but we were very lucky."

During the war years the boys helped with the chores. "Oh my word, yes, they chopped the wood and if I was in a rush for the cinema" [this was another job of Betty's, but more of that anon] "they would have their tea and I would leave them to wash up, oh yes they were good and they would do the garden. [By this time they had moved to a different part of the town.] See, we had a garden what dad had done which was right down to the railway line. We planted sprouts and fruit and everything. You know we had yellow gooseberries in the hedge. Coo, they used to eat like grapes, beautiful, and the celery buried in the soot that was really good stuff and we had three lovely apple trees, little red ones, you could polish them on a cloth and they would shine! In fact, I think the boys sold the greengrocer some of them we had so many. It was better than them laying rotten, they didn't get much for them but it was a bit of pocket money wasn't it? They used to go rabbiting in the harvest field and then they went and collected – what was it the W.I. was asking for? – not the berries, the hips, they used to get four or five sandbags full of them. That took some picking in a week and they took them along and got a few shillings. If there was anything going they volunteered for it, which was lovely because they didn't have pocket money in them days. They would turn their hand to anything, well almost, dad would say, 'Who's going out tonight? Mr F.'s coming with his horse and cart so I want some more manure for the tomatoes.'

'I don't like doing that.'

'I can't help that, it's for the tomatoes, you'll eat them.'

"So they used to go with the shovel. They took it in turns when the manure was about; they had to go. One of them took a pail in a carrier bag so nobody would see. Dad used to say, 'You can't be proud, we've all got to do our bit.'"

In May 1940 there was a real threat of invasion and Churchill announced the formation of the Local Defence Volunteers, later to be called the Home Guard. By that time most men had been called up and were in the forces; the Home guard attracted those left at home, the young, the older men and those in reserved occupations, all from different walks of life. Betty's father, who as she has said was gassed during the 14-18 war, was keen to do his duty.

"Dad was a Home Guard, he'd go out twice a week for practice. Anyway a boy lived next door, he was in the army. When he was home he would take me to the pictures on a Saturday afternoon; I wasn't very old then, only 11 or 12. He was home on leave and he'd been out with a couple of the boys and of course he wasn't used to having a drink and his Mum was mad with him. I mean, a man who was fighting for his country. He'd been out with his uniform on and he had to go back on Sunday night. He come to the wall and said, 'I'll get wrong when I go back, Bett.'

'What's happened?'

'I've lost a button off my tunic.'

'Oh dear. Wait a minute I'll go and see if it is the same size as on dad's Home Guard coat.'

Dad was at work, so I went and nipped it off and sewed it on his tunic. I didn't think a lot but he went away happy. When practice night come, dad put on his uniform and then his coat, 'That' a rum'un', he say. 'I must have lost a button.'

'You have dad, I'll get you one tomorrow.' It cost me a halfpenny. So that was a little white lie but I got through it and done a good turn and nobody was any the wiser."

By the time Betty was 16 she had two different jobs." At 2 o'clock I used to bike over to Geldeston where I was nursemaid to twins. I was still looking after the boys so I couldn't get a full time job, so I used to bike over there from 2–6 p.m., come home and get their tea, change and wash and get up to the cinema at 7 p.m. where I was an usherette. I went round with a tray selling ice cream, cigarettes and lollipops. Lollipops were a penny and we used to make them under the stage on a Friday night ready for the children at Saturday afternoon matinee, all colours, all a penny. You got this powder stuff, put them all in these trays and they freeze, and you lay the stick in and it goes in the lolly. Then I had the poor old boys from the workhouse at Shipmeadow. They used to come in on a Wednesday afternoon, and I used to make sure that I kept them seats. So when the young lads used to come in on a Saturday night from the country, I gave them a paper bag and said, 'When you light your cigarettes up just have three draws and put them in the bag.'

'What you want them for, are you going to roll your own Betty?'

'No, they're for my lads from the workhouse.'

"I done that every Saturday night so that Wednesday when they come in I said to the one in charge, 'Here you are, if you break them up when you get back and share the tobacco out you shall have a cigarette.'

"I felt so sorry for 'em. They were all ages, 30s, 40s, 50s, they had nothin', half a crown a week they were allowed. They were in the workhouse, down and outs; they had their keep and that half a crown was their pocket money. They all knew Betty. About ten used to come, they'd walk in and back again. I said to the boys at summertime, 'You can bring me a few apples in [for the workhouse men] and they used to take a bag back with them. The manager said, 'You look after all the strays.' I say, 'Yes, it's a pity there aren't a few more like me.' He wouldn't give them nothing. Noooooo. He was a hard man, very selfish man. He was a proper chain smoker and like a drop of whisky, he used to pop over to the Bear & Bells and leave me there on my own. I didn't worry about that. I had a nice woman in the cashier desk, and if she had a night off I used to go in and help at the desk, so I was an all-rounder."

On one occasion when Betty had been left alone. "When they had started and the boys were upstairs operating the films they said to me, 'What about some fish and chips, Betty?' so I went to Bond's and got them some and when I come back I could hear them all stamping their feet in the cinema, so I runned upstairs. I said, 'What are you doin' ? You're running the picture upside down.' That was a cowboy, I don't know how they thought they were going to shoot anyone! They were playing cards and they didn't realise that they had put the next reel in upside down.

'Get that changed they're all down there stamping their feet.'

'We didn't hear nothing.'

'No, you're concentrating on that blinking card game.'

"Then 'cause I got commission on what I sold on my tray and I was relying on that. They stuck such a stupid little torch on the tray and you know how you are trying to hold your tray and trying to hold the torch to give the change, well that was my excuse, I said to him [the manager], 'I'm not pleased with that torch, I'm nervous I'm going to give them the wrong change.' Well, it weren't that, 'cause I wanted to sell my stuff didn't I? So he sent me off to get the torch I wanted, coo it had a beam like a saucer! Well you know Saturday nights you get the young couples at the back, I stand there 'Ice Cream – Cigarettes'."

'For God's sake sort her out, move her down,' and when half time come in the interval they say, 'Look out she's round again!'

"Well I'd sold out before I got half way down. Coo I didn't half get good commission. So the manager come through, he was over the other side, he said, 'That torch is strong,' and I said, 'I know it is, I know now I shan't give wrong change.' I was the devil, oh the fun of growing up!"

Betty was not only quick-witted she certainly wasn't work-shy, because not only was she going to Geldeston in the afternoons to care for the two children and her evening cinema work, she suddenly mentions her early start at the beginning of the day – "And then at half past six in the morning I used to go and open up [the cinema] and clean up with a couple of other women who came in at seven and I knocked off about quarter to nine. We used to have a broom each and you would meet in the middle of the seats when you sweep up. I had poor Miss Ward, she was 29 and I was 16. I had a night off that night and when I went in the morning I had three pails full of cartons an' that and I looked at her and she only had one.

'Did they all sit on my side last night?'

'I don't know, Betty.'

'It looks like they did I've got three here.'

"I thought I'm going to watch you tomorrow. In the morning I let her get started and then I went in, so I caught her up in the second row. What she done, she took her broom to the middle and she just pushed it like that. I said 'What do you think you're doing, Dolly? I might be young and you might be older than me, but that is a naughty thing what you're doing, you're a Salvation Army woman, you should know different.'

'Oh,' she said, 'that's how you do it isn't it?'

'No, hold you hard, I'll get next door to the next row and I'll show you how it's done.' So, I got one of the other women, 'Come on we're just going to sweep this row to show Dolly how it's done.' And she see how we parted each way.

"I was still at home house-keeping for the boys and there was just a bit of money on the end of it for me, a few bits for myself, if you know what I mean, and the boys, 'cause dad's money weren't big and they could have a few little extras. Then dad got a job nearer home on the drome or in the town, he used to walk everywhere. He was slim and tall and he used to eat well and he always used to have his hot dinner. I used to take him either a beef puddin' or a stew, he didn't have sandwiches, because by the time he got home he didn't want a heavy meal, he'd sooner have it like that, then have a light tea to go to bed on. From home I used to bike up there, I had one of those high handle-bars bike, so I done his puddin' and I wrapped it up well in the greaseproof and a tea cloth and then I put a towel round it; I'm glad I did, as I come down Grove Hill, I had one of the apple baskets, because we used to have the apples and I had it on the flippin handle bars and that touched the wheel and when I got to the bottom of the hill when my knee touched that the puddin' jumped out, that went over the wall and I thought, 'Oh my puddin' my puddin'!' and I had grazed my knee, well naturally coming off. Mrs Jenner run out and we picked it up and wrapped it all round and I took it to dad. I picture him with his mates sitting out there, 'Here comes your girl.' He said, 'You're late,' then he see my knee. 'What have you done?' When I told him I'd come off my bike, he told me to get home and get that washed and looked after. So, tea time when he got back, he always went to the wash house and have a rinse before he come in to have something else to eat. He sat down and he looked at me and I knew he was itching to say something, so I said, 'Was your beef puddin' alright dad?'

'Well my dear, there were more stones in that than there is on Yarmouth beach, but I didn't break a tooth.'

"When you look back he always had a hot meal, beef puddins, stews, a sausage pattie, anything what I made at home that would be ready for the boys when they come out of school, he had at lunch time. That's why he had the strength to do everything what he done. He was gassed during the first world war bless him but he didn't let that stop him. He was only out of work once, they stood him off when all the men came off one road surface job because they had lost the contract and he said, 'I've got to sign on, Betty, Thursday.' He wouldn't go to sign on till there weren't anyone in the queue, that's how he felt and thank goodness he was only a fortnight and he was into work. That was the only time I'd ever known him out of work. He didn't like that, so degrading.

"Brother Jim had left school at 14 yrs. when our Mother died and our grandparents managed to get him an apprenticeship at the printing works in Bungay, which gave him a start but meant that there was no extra money coming into the family. For his National Service he opted to be a Bevin boy in the mines. Then Dad was taken very ill at home with gall stones. I was 16 yrs., and Dr McClaren said, 'It's no goo, my lassie, you'll have to get your older brother home to give you a hand.' I hadn't been up the town for six weeks, I was nursing my dad. You could have got your fist in dad's stomach and he didn't want to go into hospital, so we kept him at home, and that's when the doctor came in every day, but he was really ill. They didn't operate, not then they didn't; and then the doctor got tough with the mines and they said yes, Jim could come home on compassionate leave. He came home and then after dad felt better and up and about that gave me a chance to do a bit of shopping and that. The boys had done all the running about, Charlie and Dennis, and then Jim went back again and finished his two years. He came back to Beccles then."

Each of the other boys in turn left school, found a job and did their National Service. "None of them were lazy. They were grafters, they really were." Betty continued to care for the family as well as working at her various jobs. Then she met Bill…

"When I was biking to Geldeston as a nurse maid, I passed Darby's [wood yard] and they were bringing a log across the road. He said 'Hello', I said 'Hello', just like that and carried on. Then every afternoon after dinner he always seemed to be out at the gate there. Then he said, 'Can I have a date?'

'Yeh, might as well,' I said. Well you know me, 'course I was working at the cinema. His mother was a Londoner, but his father was a Beccles chap. Bill's father was born in the house by the river that we went to all those years later. Isn't it funny how we got in with each other like that? His father was at the gas works, a stoker. We went up the Regal [this was the other, rather better, cinema in the town] that was my only night off. I was 18, nearly 19, I think. Well having three brothers, they said, 'Well who is he?' and everything else. I told them that he was a very nice lad. Because you see Bill was 29 yrs., he was just nine and a half years older than me. My Father said that when they are older they are more sensible. Dad took to him right from the start and the boys did; thought the world of him. My brothers were thrilled to death. He took me home one night and my dad knew that Bill's Father had a lot of garden and Bill had been talking about a garden fork, so dad said, 'I've got two in my shed, you're most welcome to one.' This was ten o'clock at night and he got stopped by the police going past the police station, they wanted to know where he had been and where he was going. We always laughed about that. We married at St. Michael's, I was just 20, and had the reception at the Cambridge Inn up Northgate. My dad give me away, weren't he proud! And I kept worrying, 'I don't know if I'm ready to get married, I'm leaving you.' 'Cause I had to leave Dennis and Charlie at home you see, because Jim was married, and I felt for them. Dad said, 'You've done all you can do, Betty, now you've got your life.' But after I got married I used to go up there every day nearly, and sort the washing out and done them some baking. I carried on and Bill never minded. No, you couldn't just leave them like that."

Betty's Father had two sisters who were very settled living in their own bungalow and working in a hotel in Newcastle. In their fifties they decided it was time to come home and nurse their elderly parents as well as keeping an eye on their brother. So at last some of that responsibility was taken off Betty's shoulders. "That was about a year before they came, but then they took over and looked after dad right until he died."

Betty and her Bill settled into their home by the river which was rented from Darby's where Bill worked. "We went straight in there. It was either that or a Nissen hut up the drome. So, we worked like mad on that and got that nicely. We were there at Riverside 17 or 18 years and we had two children. I used to do the catering for the carnival then because every year the events were outside Riverside House – swimming, Miss Waveney, decorated boats and the greasy pole. The girls, just 2 and 4 years old, used to help their dad greasing the pole in the morning and then I done the catering. We had Ken Dodd, Lennie Lion, George Formby and a few others. I used to drop a list of what I was doing into Ernie S. [who was in charge of that side of the carnival], and he used to bring it down and tell me it was alright for the guests and the Mayor and Mayoress. At Riverside we had a bath in our kitchen with a big long table on top of it. Bill had just got in the bath and the doorbell went, we only had that one door, so I shut the lid down and said, 'You'll breathe.'

Ernie come to the door, 'Here's your order lass.'

'Thank you ever so much I'll see you up the office tomorrow to confirm it.'

'Right.'

'You don't mind if I go?'

'Oh no,' he said, he must have thought I was ever so rude, but I was just thinking of poor Bill under there!

"I took in boarders at Riverside for about seven years. I thought I can't go out and leave the children so I'll bring the work in, which I did. Then I looked after Hipperson's four houseboats outside ours up the Cut. I done that for years and then I went in the boatyard and when I retired I'd been on that yard for 36 years. I got a nice bouquet and a necklace and a buffet with a bottle of champagne and in the Journal 'Betty

Sails Into Retirement.' Beautiful. I was home a fortnight when I was asked to help someone out in their home. I had another week off and then I went on a month's trial and I was there eleven and a half years. I finished when Bill was brought home from the quay with a stroke. I was 70."

From the age of ten Betty didn't stop working and caring for family and many others along the way. The maiden aunts who came home from Newcastle took some of her old responsibilities off her shoulders while she embarked on married life and started a family, but as they aged it was to an ever willing Betty they turned to for extra support. Once again she was running errands from one end of the town to the other on her little legs! Her Bill she kept at home and nursed for many years.

It is Betty's own words that best sum up her family and attitude to life: "They were all happy, we never had no split-ups in the family, nothing like that; and I think that's what makes you how you are today, I do honestly. I mean different bits people say like, 'You've always got a smile.' Well, I said, that get you through life, no one want to know if you're miserable. I said that in't 'cause I've had an easy life."

"Well, I always feel better for meeting you."

"They all say that."

9

DENNIS

FROM SUFFOLK COUNTRY LANES TO THE WORLD; ONE MAN'S WAR...

An unobtrusive avuncular man, Dennis is generally a one of few words but when he speaks it is with thought and meaning. For years he ran a considerable building business, was known as a good and considerate employer and cared greatly for the community of which he was a part. When he spoke to me about his life he was in his 91st year, physically slowing down but as articulate as ever.

"I have my family tree on my father's side dating from 1698 and my forbears were all either builders or farmers, husbandmen as they were called in those days. Some of them prospered, some of them didn't. I suppose the easiest to talk about is my great grandfather Thomas who was a builder with a building business in Barford in Norfolk. Don't know much about him, but he had a reputation for enjoying his drink and also for having a very clever pony which would take him home when he was intoxicated in the evening. He must have devoted too much time to drinking because his business went bankrupt. He had four sons who were in the business with him; when he died they decided they would pay off their Father's debts, so they split up and each went his own way.

George went to America, Harry went to Harleston and started a business there and Herbert and the other brother came to Beccles and started a building business in 1900."

This was a shrewd move on the part of the two brothers. Although Barford was only 7 miles from Norwich the village was small with a population of just over 300 people. In comparison Beccles was a veritable metropolis with a population of nearly 7,000 souls. It was an ancient market town situated on the River Waveney which was still navigable up to the town for vessels of 100 tons so there was considerable traffic and it was on the East Suffolk line of the Great Eastern Railway. A number of businesses thrived there, notably Clowes Printing Works, several maltings and an agricultural implements works. It had its own hospital and courthouse and the popular livestock market brought people in from the surrounding district. Years ago an elderly man described it as a 'wild west town' because of the number of pubs and the unruly nightlife! Obviously the new builders arriving in the town saw the possibility for growth.

"Their first yard was down by the river, where the boatyard is now and the first house they built was a large property near the town centre. They did a lot of building on the Raveningham Estate for the Bacon family, including one of the several schools which they built in the area. The Maltings at Ditchingham, that has recently been destroyed by fire, they built them too. My grandfather built most of the houses in Grove Road, from the top to the bottom. Then in the early 1900's he built a pair of houses there which is where my grandmother lived and he built this house to please her. It was typically Edwardian; incidentally, in my opinion the Edwardian era was one of the best times for building. I think a lot of good quality work was done in Edwardian times as against the Georgian times. Anyhow, he built this house for my grandmother and had what was then considered the modern things. Apart from the kitchen range, in the kitchen she had a soft water pump, which she could pump indoors and there was a well outside which had a pump so they had a continuous supply of soft water over the sink. They had a boiler of course, they had a bathroom, a modern bathroom, a toilet upstairs and down, and the whole place was painted white. In Victorian times white was the colour for everything; it seems to have come full circle because it is now the popular colour for paintwork inside. In the hall there were tessellated tiles all various patterns and colours. Attics upstairs; I remember the attics because when I was a boy, attached to the house there was an orchard, and when the apples were ripe it was my job to pick them, carry them upstairs to the attic and lay them out on paper. I had to lay them out so they didn't touch the others. That was one of my jobs, the other was to cut sticks. Also atttached to the house there was an outside toilet and a stick shed because there were coal fires then and they needed a constant supply of sticks for my grandmother to light the fires. My grandmother was an excellent cook; she always cooked a dinner for me and I particularly liked her Yorshire puddings. I do mine now individually; she did hers on a flat tin and they were lovely, a flat tin I suppose 6 x 9 inches and cut them into pieces and oh they were lovely. I remember Christmas time, my grandmother had five children, after the First War there seemed to be a dearth of children, I don't know why it was, perhaps birth control had been discovered. Of her five children only two of them had any family. My uncle up the garage had no children, my aunt Elsie had no children, my uncle Harry had no children, my father had four and his sister had two daughters. Christmas time was always something special, they all got together and they all made a fuss of the children because they had none of their own. I think their lives had been empty for them because they were missing something."

As Dennis mentioned, his grandfather and great uncle arrived in the Suffolk border town of Beccles around 1900. "What happened was that my father was apprenticed to Brook Marine [boatbuilders] of Lowestoft. He used to cycle from Redisham [a village outside Beccles] the 11½ miles to Oulton Broad every day. When he finished his apprenticeship, he must have been about twenty, the war had broken out and he joined up and he was in the Suffolk Hussars, which was a mounted regiment then, they had horses. There was a shortage of shipwrights, boat builders, so he was taken out of the army and sent to Southampton where he worked in a boatyard called Divell & Sons, which is still there, I've seen the yard. He became foreman and whilst he was there he met and seduced the lady who was working in the office, Elsie, who was my mother. She was 17 yrs. at that time I suppose. So they were obliged to get married when she was 18 yrs. old and then they had their first child who was my brother. I was born two years later, so by the time my mother was 20 yrs. she had two children. Yes, I was born in 1920. Two years later Father decided to come back to Beccles and join his father in the building business so they moved back and had a council house in Weston [a small village about 3 miles from the market town], where I lived for just over 2 years. I don't remember anything about this. They said I got very muddy and played about in the ditches. My mother told me that she had to push the pram with her two children into Beccles to do the shopping and then push it back and one day she bought some kippers for my father's tea and as she was pushing the pram back my brother and I ate them up. That time must have been very hard for her because she was so young and she wasn't very big and she'd got two children living in the country which she hadn't been used to. After the First War there was a need for houses and the government's solution was to give a subsidy to builders; I don't know how much it was in financial terms but I know that my grandfather said that he built two houses for the price of one with the aid of the subsidy."

The family then moved into a new house in the town. Today it is a built-up area but when they moved in, "There was a hockey pitch opposite and where the big council estate is beyond that now there were just fields. What I remember about that area was the east winds blowing across from the North Sea, I had short trousers and my knees used to get frozen, oh the wicked wind! I hate the east winds, I still do. The new house had a triplex stove, if you know what they are, they're like a built-in range, which is not a back boiler. The house was modern in that we had a bath but it was in the kitchen. It was covered by a table which dropped down; but we had a bath and not many people had one in1927. I don't remember helping my mother very much to be honest, I don't think I was very kind to my mother on reflection. That's a cause of regret now but I mean that's not something you realise when you are young.

"First of all I went to the council school, I suppose it wasn't a very good school as my father took me away and I went to the National School, I had a year there. I couldn't write very well, so Mr Watkis, the headmaster, he taught me how to write. I was in a class of 40 I think, the first term I came 30th, the second term I came 30th, the third term I came top. I got a scholarship that year and went to the Leman School when I was twelve. My brother was already there, he was a paying pupil and I was a scholarship boy. I don't remember much about it until the second day when I got involved in a fight. There was a boy called Bobby Throgmorton. I don't know why it happened or how it happened, but he was bigger than me and two years older, but he had a go at me and something happened, we had a tussle and he got beaten. My mother had a letter from his father demanding to know why his son had been ill-treated by this boy and in the process his glasses had been broken. He wanted my mother to pay for them. I'll always remember the letter because it was signed Robert Throgmorton, Captain Royal Navy (Retired). I don't know what happened but that was my first introduction to the school. Anyhow, I was there from 1932–1937. I liked algebra and mathematics, I wasn't particularly good at English, French I managed. I was no good at woodwork but then the man who taught me was no good either; he hadn't got a clue really, I could see he had no idea what he was talking about. I suppose on reflection I did fairly well at school, I wasn't the brightest but out of a class of 17 in my last year I was 3rd. I got a good school certificate with matriculation, I was Head Prefect and also Captain of Cricket and Victor Ludorum for two years. So I had a fairly successful year. One memory: in 1934 we were in class and a teacher came in and brought two new girls into the classroom, saying, 'This is Molly Moyes and Myrtle Wardley' and that's the first time I saw my wife! I don't know why but we were attracted to each other straight away and that's how it was for the rest of our lives really. In those days you were not expected to talk to girls, or girls talk to boys, there were school rules. You shouldn't walk out together, you shouldn't eat sweets, you should always wear your hat and you should raise your hat to a master – all these thing applied. I had to go before the Headmaster and was reprimanded for trying to give the school a bad name as I had been seen talking to Molly. Didn't make any difference apparently. So that's how I met my wife. The only girlfriend all my life, which is sad when it comes to this, isn't it?

"What I do remember about the Leman School was the homework. Suddenly when you started there you got homework; we hadn't considered that before and it was quite a thing because it stopped all your other activities. I belonged to Scouts; I was patrol leader of the Peewits but I had to give it up because you just couldn't fit it in. We used to go camping and one year we went in for the Suffolk competition, we sewed our own rucksacks and helped to make our tents."

Dennis at the age of seven and his older brother were encouraged to join the church choir. "My brother was musical, he played the piano, I was not musical at all but I had a good memory so whereas my brother read music I sang from memory. I was head choir boy when I finished and I sang solo but then my voice broke early and I left. We had morning service at 11 a.m. and evening service at 6.30 p.m; we had choir practice on Mondays for the boys and mixed practice for the whole choir on Friday nights. And we got paid! I think we got about 3d a time, something like that, we got paid quarterly. I remember on one occasion when Dr Woodhill's daughter got married, there were twelve boys went to sing and he gave the choir boys £2, so we split it up and had 3s 4d each, which was tremendous. In those days the church was a much more profitable establishment, they could afford to employ a choir master and an organist and they paid a full time verger."

During his childhood Dennis' father was working long hours. "Let me tell you about the generation he grew up in. In those days the men would work and they would come home, their wives would feed them and then they would wash and change and go off to the pub or the club for the night. That was their life. That was the life that my father was brought up in and that was the life that he tended to lead; he didn't stay at home at night, he always went out." Consequently there was not a close relationship between father and son. "However, I was in business with my father. We were business partners for years and had complete trust in each other. When I left school there was no careers guidance, no careers structure at all but everyone who left the Leman School at that time had a job. Many of them went to be civil servants in the post office, Air

Ministry and all sorts of things like that, teaching and so on. I went into building. I wasn't asked, just told. It was decided for me so that's what I did. I don't think I was particularly suited. My older brother went into the civil service. Started off at the Post Office, then after the war he studied and trained as a librarian. But it was decided that I should go into building. In the holidays my father used to give me work with the men. That's how you learn, isn't it? I don't know that I particularly wanted to but you don't have a choice do you?" In response to the question 'Any thoughts as to what you would have liked to do?' without hesitation came the reply, "Medicine. First of all you had to have Latin and then you had to have a lot of money [he laughs] – I didn't have either. I got matriculation, I could have gone to university but I didn't have the need. So I started about 1937. I didn't know anything so I went to night school at Yarmouth and I spent a lot of time on correspondence courses, learn what I could there and then I had to pick up what I could. Not the ideal way to start. My father should have sent me away somewhere and had me trained. So I had to pick it up as I went along. Perhaps that's the best way to learn because if you make a mistake you don't forget it, do you?

"That was in 1937 and I joined up in 1940 – I volunteered. I thought to myself, 'There's a war going on and it's history in the making, I ought to be a little piece of it, just a little bit, I don't expect I shall do very much but at least I will be a bit of it.' I couldn't get into flying because of my eyesight but I joined the Air Force. First of all I went to Uxbridge to be sworn in, then I went home until I was called up on 23rd December 1940. I went to Cardington where I was put in a billet with a crowd of other fellows who I had never seen before and on Christmas Eve I was inoculated, vaccinated, fitted with clothes which didn't fit and put in a billet of all these strange men. On Christmas Day I woke up with a sore arm, feeling ill and I put on all these rough clothes and sat down to Christmas dinner with people I didn't know and not feeling very hungry. Anyhow, I got over that and I went to Bridgnorth and did some training there, square bashing, discipline and so on. Then I went to a place in Wiltshire where I had six weeks to be trained as an armourer. When I was tossed out of there I had a week's leave which I will never forget. [Obviously the experience of being away from home for the first time combined with an introduction to military life had not been entirely enjoyable!] Then I went to Pershore in Worcestershire to an airfield where they were flying Wellingtons and training aircrew for Bomber Command. I was there for the summer. Whilst I was there we used to get leave, about 48 hours. By that time Molly was living at Wymondham, she was at the Food Office there. As there was rationing during the war the Food Office was where the people who gave out coupons and ration books worked so I used to hitch hike to Wymondham, the only way to get there actually. Hitch-hiking was quite a thing in the war; I could go from Worcestershire to Wymondham in 6 hours. I could do it quite easily knowing where to stand and where to stop. Didn't always work out though. I remember one night, I got out late and I got as far as Bedford, no, Northampton one night it got dark and there was no one about and I couldn't get any lifts so I started to walk and I met up with a couple of other fellows, someone in the navy and a soldier, and we walked. Arrived at Wymondham at 12o'clock, had something to eat and turned round and went back again. Anyhow I was training aircrew there and servicing the aircraft. I remember one night that Bath got bombed, we could see the light. One day we had some aircraft delivered. It was a new airfield and the runways were all concrete and these aircraft were parked on the runway, there was a bright white light and there were these black aircraft on this white runway and they got bombed that night. Anyway, in the morning I was walking over there and an officer stopped me and he said, "Are you an airman?"

and I said, "Yes". He said, "Well there is an unexploded bomb there, I want you to guard it." I thought well what the hell am I going to do? So, I stood by this hole with this unexploded bomb; I just had to stand there for four hours. I don't know if I had to stop anyone going there but a sign would have done.

"When it came to December men were being drafted overseas. They went in ones and twos and the signalman had to go first of course. At the beginning of December I was told it was my time and I had fourteen days leave. I came home and we decided to get married. My father-in-law didn't agree with it but we got a special licence and got married. On reflection it wasn't a sensible thing to do but there it was, we did it, so we were married for a week and then I said goodbye to my wife. For our honeymoon we went to the Imperial Hotel in Russell Square in London for two days.

Then came Dennis' war. For the young man who had only lived in a small rural town and like many others had never been far from home, the next few years opened up unimagined horizons, introducing him to a world he had never even dreamt of experiencing.

"Anyhow, after I got married I went to Wilmslow in Cheshire which was the transit camp and there we were issued with our tropical kit, kit bags and so on. After about ten days I got on a boat at Liverpool and I remember one of the last things I saw were the Liver Birds on top of the Liver building. The boat was a New Zealand ship called the Arooha which belonged to the Shaw Savill Line. She had been used for bringing frozen meat and was converted into a troop carrier. We sailed across Belfast Bay and went into the Atlantic in January and it was rough! Oh, it was horrible. There were three thousand men on board and most of us were sick at the same time. It was horrible. In the toilets it was just swimming in vomit. We were ill. Anyway after a few days of that we felt a bit better and then as we got south the weather turned a bit, it got a bit warmer and we sat on deck. We stopped at Freetown, Africa of course. It was the first time I had a mango there. We couldn't get off the ship, they just brought them aboard and we watched these little boys. We threw coins overboard and these little boys dived under the water and stuffed them in their mouths. Then we carried on till we came to Durban. That was 14th February 1941. That was the day that Singapore fell so we knew we weren't going there. So we camped on a place called Clairwood, on the race course, idyllic, it was heaven. We had showers in the open air. You could see the spray made rainbows round your feet, it was paradise. We sat in the open with our shirts off and there were big tables and they put jars of jam on, they weren't small jars, they were 7lb jars of pineapple jam and you could help yourself. It was paradise. We only had three days. Yes it was lovely, Clairwood Racecourse. Then we got another boat called the Viceroy of India, she was an ex P&O boat. There was a big crowd on there so we ended up in the prison, the brig, which was in the bowels of the ship. I think there were four of us and it was quite comfortable really. When we washed our clothes all we had to do was get a piece of string or rope, tie our clothes on, put them through the porthole, trail them through the water and they all washed beautifully."

Disembarking at Port Taufiq at the end of the Suez Canal they went on to the transit camp before splitting up. Dennis found himself going to and fro between Nasarawa on the banks of the Nile, a place he hated [partly because the glare of the sun hurt his eyes badly] where the huge limestone caves were used for ammunition storage, and Kataba in the desert. Eventually he moved on to Kasfareet where they wanted six men to join a squadron…

"Six of us were sent. I was the Leading Aircraftman so I was in charge. We went to a place called Amarna and when we got there we were told we were flying to Palestine tomorrow.

Shan't forget that, because that was when they were being pushed back into the desert and I went to the headquarters and reported there and I saw all these R.A.F. Officers. They looked so tired and worried, and I thought 'Things aren't going well.' Anyhow, we got the plane in the morning, a Wellington it was, and flew to Acacia in Palestine, paradise again. The runways were between olive groves and vineyards, oh lovely. Have you ever been to Palestine? It's a lovely little country; pity about the people but the country is nice."

They were to be the ground crew for No.10 Squadron. They had to bomb the aircraft and when they returned, wherever they landed, they had to go and do any repairs necessary.

"Then we moved down to Fayid, down the Canal. Oh, that was wicked there. We didn't have any billets there, we had some huts and outside there was just a verandah, concrete, and we had nowhere to sleep so we slept on the concrete; we got quite used to it. All we had in the world was two blankets and a ground sheet and a haversack with our change of clothes in. Shirts and shorts, that's all. Anyhow we were quite happy, we got fed alright. The thing was these aircraft, which were metal, stood in the sun all day and we had to bomb them up at 4 o'clock in the afternoon and they were like ovens. To bomb them up we had to go inside and winch these bombs up, we used to strip down to nearly nothing, we used to sweat…

"Anyhow we did that and then I got sent to another blooming place with limestone caves. Whilst I was there a posting came through for one airman for an unknown destination, so six of us drew for it and I lost. A chap called Jonnie Pahl won and I said to him, 'You don't want to go to Japan do you?'

'No, I don't think I'll go.'

'You let me have it then.'

"So he let me have it! I had to report to G.H.Q. in Cairo and they told me I was going to Station A which I found out was Ankara. In the middle of the Nile there is an island called Gazera Island and they had a camp there where I stayed for a week or so. Then I was given some money and told to go to a certain outfitters in Cairo to get some civilian clothes and a passport and so on. After a fortnight there I was in civilian clothes with two other chaps and one afternoon in October we got on a train in Cairo station and went off to Palestine and on to Ankara. We got off at Haifa and went to the Carmel Hotel at the foot of Mount Carmel and had a good lunch there. While we were there we got talking to a Major in the army who was travelling by road to Beirut and he offered us a lift. There were three of us, there was a sergeant in the Air Force and Squadron Leader Haytor, who was a New Zealander, and me. It was dark when we got to Beirut so the only place we could stay was a place called the KitKat, which was a night club really. The next morning we went to the station to continue our trip to Ankara. I'd better back-track a bit. When we began to get kitted out for the journey we had to go and collect money and various currencies because we were travelling to Palestine, Syria and Turkey and needed currency. With seniors we stood to attention. Two Wing Commanders with money in front of them and various currencies and sheets of paper where they did their travel calculations and they would write down how much money we would need to transit each country. I watched them and it occurred to me that at one stage they put a decimal point in the wrong place; because of my lowly rank, Leading Aircraft Flight, I didn't feel I could point out this error. What eventually happened was, when we went to the station in Beirut, to pay our fare to get to Ankara, we hadn't got enough money because this decimal point was indeed in the wrong place. So Hayter, who was the Squadron Leader, he was only 23 yrs., he said, 'I know how to get money'. We got a taxi and went to the Royal Australian Air Force Squadron stationed outside the town and he asked to see the Adjutant, told him who we were and what our problem was. He said, 'That's fine, you can have what you like, but you MUST sign for it. You can have whatever you like but must have a signature.'

"So we got a pocket of money each and off we went. When we got to the station we booked a sleeper to Ankara. First time I had been on a sleeper and it was part of the Orient Express. I've been on the Orient Express since but I have never seen one like that, because between dual compartments there was a shower and when you open on one you lock it on the other one. So we had a shower between us, that was heaven. We had two days of this, we were fed, it was lovely. [Dennis' war was not all discomfort by any means and he soon learnt to appreciate the finer things in life.] Got there and booked into the Tea Palace Hotel and next day we went up to the Embassy. We were met by the Air Attaché and you would have thought we were old friends.

"In a hearty voice he said, 'Good morning my fellows, how are you and have you had a good journey?'

"We weren't used to this!

'Now you must go and see the Adjutant and get some money and you must get yourselves some warm clothing.'

"The next day we went back to him and asked why we were there and what were we going to do.

'My dear chap have you seen the sights? Have you been to the Roman ruins?' We thought, well this isn't why we came here but we had a week of this. Hayter, the 23-year-old New Zealander, he had done two tours of duty in the desert, and he was a wild boy. He really was wild. His declared ambition in life was to sleep with a woman of every nationality and he was well on his way to achieving his object. And he liked his drink. The first night we were there he had a drink and he was making a nuisance of himself and we had quite a battle putting him to bed. In Ankara there is a place called Carpages which is where the international set used to meet. This is a neutral country and people from various embassies all went into this night club and glared at each other across the floor, but this was a neutral country. The German Ambassador was a man called von Papen and he had a very attractive daughter. Hayter got into this place, he had a few drinks and after a time he thought he ought to be dancing with von Papen's daughter so he staggered across the floor... he nearly created an international incident! Anyway he got sent back to Egypt fairly quickly.

"The other fellow, Sgt. Wilson, and I were sent to a port on the southern coast on the border of Syria and Turkey where we spent the winter with nothing much to do really. Sometimes if the ships came in we had to deal with the cargo, that was all. We stayed at a place owned by a Greek and were looked after by Sidica. There was a Syrian minority, basically Arabic, and they spoke French as Syria was a French Protectorate. There was this big Turkish population so these children were brought up with three languages; not only did they speak them they spoke them all at the same time. A Father would ask a child a question in one language and she would reply in another. While we were there we got to know the family, they had got a couple of boys, twins who attended school, and they were desperate to learn languages. So they had three languages, they were learning German and Italian at school and they desperately wanted to talk to us to learn English. Just imagine the background and the possibilities for boys like that. Sidica did the cooking and because I had done a little French at school I was the link with her so we managed with my schoolboy French.

"In the spring I went to a place called Katia where we were building a bomb dump. Now a bomb dump is not a building, it is just a bare piece of ground where you make a bomb dump. Perhaps I had better tell you why we were there in the first place. During the war Turkey was neutral but it accepted military aid from both sides. Part of the British aid was constructing airdromes and laying down bomb dumps, petrol stores, food stores, to equip these airfields in case they had to be moved. So there was a fatigue party formed, twenty RAF personnel and twenty Army personnel, and they were distributed around the country. When I went to Katia there were army jobbers there and we had to cope on our own. We had a communication office given to us by the railway station there, which was the only place which could send telegrams in code. We used to get 'Five George Edinburgh', which meant you had got five loads of bombs coming from somewhere. It was comical really because they were on quite open carriages for everyone to see. We had our own lorries and drivers. We had to go to the station, find out what was coming, meet it, unload it and put them in the bomb dump. It got a bit lonely at times, but we got the mail. The railway through Turkey was a single track, built by the Germans in the 1920s I suppose, quite an engineering feat because it goes through tunnels and round mountains; good system but one track. But most unreliable; it wasn't what time will the mail come but which day. We got our mail through the King's Messenger who travelled from Haifa I suppose, through to Istanbul. So if he got through at three in the morning, then you got down to the station at three in the morning to meet the mail. Anyhow it was a chance to talk to an English person. After Katia I went to Astershahia, then to Ismet on the Sea of Maramara. I had a year there.

"Then it was back to Cairo where I reported to G.H.Q. and was told I must go to M.I.T. 'What's M.I.T.?'. They said Military Intelligence Turkey, and they wanted to know if I had got any photographs. Well when I was in Turkey I bought a camera and took lots of pictures and never thought anything about it. I had to stay in Cairo another week whilst they printed my photographs, Crown Copyright – they sent me copies. Then it was back to my unit down the Canal. I had Christmas there and in the spring we went to Italy. On the boat we were fed twice a day and that was dreadful! Oh, we were hungry. There was another corporal on board with me, Roy Foot; one day he was looking through his kit bag and he fund a little jar of piccalilli. We shared that jar with our slice of bread and that's a meal I shall always remember. Then we got to Taranto, we were met by our transport who had gone ahead and we had a bully beef sandwich. I shall never forget that. Lovely. This was in 1944. We had a hard time at first, as the play progressed and they took land so where there used to be forward fighter stations there were just plots of land, anywhere where an aircraft could take off and land, a field, a piece of ground; but they needed supplying and we were supplying. We weren't in too much danger but close enough. Anyhow we went to Rimini, then on to a place on the road to Bologna. I like Italy. They're nice people, they didn't understand what war was about, they are not that sort. Once I was on leave at a camp on the Mediterranean coast, it was run by the Italian prisoners of war and they did everything. They cooked, they made musical instruments out of any thing they could salvage and formed an orchestra. They found sand of different colours and with this they built columns, turned columns, it was wonderful. They did everything in this camp."

Dennis' love affair with Italy and its people never ceased and he went back many times over the years, even after he had lost his wife and he was entering his tenth decade.

Eventually he returned to the U.K. in 1945: "I rang my wife and said I will meet you at Liverpool Street and we shall go to The Imperial Hotel in Russell Square." [Where they had spent their two day honeymoon in 1941.]

'Right, good idea.'

"I was travelling from Cheshire. I stood all the way on the train to London and I arrived with my kit bag and everything I had in the world at midnight in the blackout. I got to the Imperial Hotel, walked in and said, 'Can I have a room for the night? My wife will be joining me tomorrow.' The woman behind the desk looked at me and said, 'We don't permit women in here with servicemen.' I didn't know what to say. I looked at these Americans walking up the stairs with women who obviously were not their wives. I didn't know what was going on there! So I said, 'Alright can I stay the night?' and in the morning I scoured London for somewhere to stay and there wasn't anywhere although eventually I got into the Union Jack Club for NCOs."

As soon as Dennis was demobbed it was straight back into the family building business with his Father. The war had left Britain with a severe housing shortage so he didn't have time to consider his options. The rest of his working life was already laid out for him. No longer a lowly Leading Aircraftman, he set about building up the family business so that his firm's name became synomonous with a well trained workforce and high standards. However, Dennis' overseas service opened up a whole new world for him, so much so that seventy years later he could still remember with wonder the rainbow colours with the sun shining through the water in the shower in South Africa.

10
JANET

Janet was a familiar figure at the organ in the small Norman church with no tower and that is where I first met her. She was in her late eighties then, a tiny frame with not a spare ounce of flesh on her, bright eyes and thin wispy white hair with a centre parting pulled back into a bun. Janet's organ playing had started over eighty years earlier when as a child she had had a few formal piano and organ lessons. She played with gusto on a difficult machine and the competition in that tiny church between the small congregation and their very special organist as to who would finish first and loudest was always a delight to me and I'm sure to the Lord as well. It was only sad that as the years progressed Janet's confidence waned and she worried about the occasional wrong note which didn't worry her following one iota. It just made the challenge more interesting. She always reminded me of a sparrow, erratic and quick in her movements on those spindly legs and her sentences were disjointed, always hopping from one subject to another and liberally smattered with "Oh dear" or "My dear".

When I first called at her tiny terraced bungalow in the small village surrounded by fields and just a step from the church, the floor was covered with old photographs and the odd newspaper cutting which she had got out in readiness for my visit. Before, I left a whole new tin of biscuits was brought out and a large newly baked sponge; then I discovered that she wouldn't be eating before bed and at 7 p.m. I was keeping her up anyway. Real country hospitality. This is the story of her early years, much of it in her own words.

Situated in eastern Norfolk, a land of light and vast skies, between Norwich and Great Yarmouth, Acle was a town surrounded by marshes where in the late 18th and early 19th centuries the wildfowlers had thrived. By the second half of the 1700s many of the marshes were drained. In that period there were at least thirty drainage mills in that great triangle of marsh between Acle, Yarmouth and Reedham. This meant that over a hundred years later Janet's father had marshes for grazing and good arable land. Later, the excavation in 1948 of what was thought to have been a salt pan next to the Acle New Road found early medieval pottery but the area had been populated long before that as the odd isolated coin belonging to Boadicea's great Iceni tribe had been found at Acle.

Acle New Road, built in 1831 to facilitate better communication between Norwich and Yarmouth, was by the beginning of the 20th century not the dangerous place that it had become in the 1950s and 60s when there were frequent accidents as cars multiplied and got faster, finding distance and speed difficult to gauge along this long straight road over the flat marshes. When Janet was born at the family's farm just off this road in 1906 horse-drawn vehicles still outnumbered the motorised ones. In those days Acle, as with so many market towns, was largely self-sufficient. You would find every trade from baker, butcher and draper to the stone mason, plumber and builder. The auction house, still there today, had its cattle market and, of course, there were all the allied occupations that befitted a farming area – the wheelwright, steam miller, poultry-dealer, blacksmith, corn and pollard-dealer and so forth. Tourism was coming to the area. The Angel with Bridge House was not only a public house and the home of the coal merchant but you could hire pleasure boats from there too. The King's Head had livery stables and the Queen's Head boasted a bowling green and was also the headquarters of the Cyclists Touring Club. There were two surgeons and the Medical Officer of Health and Public Vaccinator for the district were based in the town as was the District Surveyor. Sub-branches of the Capital and Counties Bank and Barclays opened every Thursday between 2 p.m. and 4.30 p.m. Meanwhile in Great Yarmouth, which was becoming a favoured seaside resort, its wealth still looked to the sea and the herring trade. On Sundays when the fishermen stayed at home you could walk across the full width of the River Yare on the trawlers moored there and when the boats came in a whole basket of herring could be bought on the quay for a shilling [5p]. Much of the what was produced from around Acle would have been brought in to sell at Yarmouth market, so the New Road was a boon linking two very different economies.

Janet's family were Yarmouth folk; her grandmother's brother was a butcher in King Street,

"There were seven in that family; four lived, two sons and two daughters. Now, my grandmother, she lived over the Brunswick Hotel in King Street, opposite St. George's Church. I was the second one of six. No seven, I forgot I had another sister, she died of diphtheria. We still lived on the Acle New Road and she went to school at St. Andrew's in Yarmouth, along the Quay." [This was an infant school accommodating around 130 children.] "Phillips, they kept the pawn shop, they were the ones that started it off in the school. Their twins were at the school and she sat between the two of them, they both died. A lot of children died. They were taken in the fever van to the hospital and if it was found that any of those children came from outside of Yarmouth they wouldn't take them, and we were. She died, she was only five years old. As they wouldn't admit her to the hospital Dr

Meadows used to come every day. Miss Platten was the school mistress. I can remember that every year my mother used to send her a bunch of flowers to remember my little sister"

Smallpox, scarlet fever and diptheria, three of the seriously infectious diseases to be feared at the beginning of the 20th century. Isolation, often known as Fever Hospitals had become common by this time and were not to be phased out until antibiotics and immunisation became readily available after the Second World War. The Fever Hospital which Janet's sister was initially taken to had been built beside Yarmouth's workhouse and although it was run by the Borough Council and not the Poor Law Union it was still tainted with the fear of being sent to such a place.

"Father was a tenant farmer; yes, arable and marshes too. There was the River Bure and the marshes went up to the farm and then up towards Thrigsby and Stokesby. My brother Horace worked on the farm, it was hard work. Chadd from Lowestoft owned the farm, Mrs Chadd's mother I think. When we moved they sold it. Oh, we used to get the scythe, my dear, and go round the headlands, and my brother used to start one side and I the other if I felt like it. I used to feed the chickens. Then once when mother was having one of the children, the last one, they had a nurse with her because she was ill then, she should never have had it, but still we couldn't help that. We had a lot of turkey chicks in the springtime and I had no end of them to look after and as they came to hatch I used to run upstairs to show mother. Then there was a thunderstorm once, I can remember, it teemed, and all these little fluffy things I had to gather them up otherwise they would have been drowned. Another time grandfather and grandmother Howell, they lived right opposite St. George's Church in Gt. Yarmouth, they had come for a holiday at ours, it was going to rain and grandmother was alone with us children, and she came along a long passageway upstairs, and then there was a flight of stairs went down into the living room there, and then if she had kept coming along, which is what she intended doing and my bedroom was along there, so she came along this one she took the first turn which was the back stairs and she went down the stairs, she split her head open. They had to send for Dr Meadows, in King Street. She lived just a few days. Her whole scalp came off."

Janet and her brother Horace were sent to the Priory School in Great Yarmouth, near the great parish church of St. Nicholas. "There used to be a chandler's shop right at the corner, Seals I think the name was, they had all sorts of things. There was a Mr Silas at the school and there was the other one who was very strict. He had a daughter and a son, lost his wife, lived at Southtown way. His son went to the Grammar School, he left him at the Priory churchyard and gave him so long to get to the school and the daughter to the High School. Oh, he was terrible, I think he was dismissed from the school for cruelty to children. Grey, I think his name was, Dr Grey."

"We were eight miles from Yarmouth. Dad used to supply some of his milk wholesale, he used to go with a horse and cart to Caister, Goff & Son. He used to take the milk to them." At first Janet used to go with her Father in the mornings and from Caister used to catch the tram into Yarmouth across The Plain. "Coming home I used to catch the tram into Caister and I used to have to walk the six miles home. Then I got a bike." Riding a bicycle did not come naturally to Janet. "I used to fall off and I used to put it against a gate, so that if I fell over that way... then I used to have to walk and push it. We were lucky because another sister went to the Priory and another one to Southern House, a private school along The Drive."

She had singing lessons at the Priory with Dr Haydon Hare. "He was very strict, you had to open your mouth wide for every syllable and if you spoke during one of his lessons you were expelled from school. One girl was sent home and she never did come back. When I was at Acle I had an organ at home, I went for organ lessons to Miss Jary, Jary's the undertakers, the eldest daughter, Lily, and she took people and I learnt there for some time and then she gave up and she recommended me to Mr Chapman in Anson Road, Southtown. A little short man, oh he was strict. When I went to Miss Jary I used to play the Bluebells of Scotland and he asked me what I could play and I played it all wrong, out of time and everything but she wasn't a professional teacher. I did that on Saturday mornings out of school hours. When we moved to Runham they got me to play the organ because my friend said, 'I know Janet can play the organ she's got one at home.' I was just about 12 years old when we went over there. We moved on the Saturday and on the Sunday I was asked to play the organ in the chapel even though I didn't know anything about the organ there so, of course, I had to go along. That's how I came to leave the church; the church at Runham needed to be restored. I played at the chapel until I was ready to leave home and went to London as a children's nurse.

"When I left school I helped mother with this, that and the other until my other sister, Grace, grew up."

Apparently the lot of being mother's help did not appeal to sister Grace and she found herself a job in the office of a butcher in Yarmouth, where she stayed until she married and then had a grocery shop with her husband. Eventually at around the age of 16 Janet started her first job, whilst still helping her mother at home. She found a place as a children's nanny.

"I didn't go to college but I knew what to do from helping with all our children. If I could get temporary work I would go there because that was where the money was. That's how I made my money." It seemed quite easy for her to find work as she was recommended by one family to another. "I started teaching John Wharton at Thrigby, preparing him for school; he eventually went to a Lowestoft school when he was about eight years old. His mum and dad, they were farmers, used to go into Yarmouth on a Wednesday and I used to let him have a little break, about ten minutes." The farm was adjacent to the house and on one occasion John took advantage of his break from lessons to go down to the farm with a fork and dig around a bit. He ignored Janet's call and when she went to find him he lashed out with the fork and stabbed her head.

"The maid said, 'You had better get on your bike and go home.' Then Mr Wharton he came down and said, 'My word I'll treat him, he won't come out for his break any more, he can keep indoors.' I was there about a year. That was my first job after I left school, I got about 15s [75p] a week, good money. The other girls were only getting about 5s [25p]."

Janet's friends had already found positions in London and by the age of eighteen this country girl who had never been very far afield went to join them. "After that I went to Queen's Gate Gardens, Kensington. I went by train all by myself, had a big old trunk, the old tin trunk is in the shed now."

Just imagine her first impressions of the city, from rural Norfolk, with very few cars on the roads, to London streets packed with a mix of motor and horse-drawn traffic, the policemen on point duty and all the trams, a throng of activity quite new to our country lass.

"I don't know who met me. Mrs Sylvester, that was my lady, had lost her husband, had one little boy, Patrick. She used to rent her house out; there was a Miss Skeat and her brother, they had an apartment, she used to rent the rooms out to different people, that's how she got her living. She was very, very nice. There were seven or eight other staff, one came from Scotland, she was the kitchen maid, but, oh she was homesick. She was crying, so Mrs Sylvester said would I mind taking her out with me for a walk, see if we can get her over her homesickness; but, she couldn't bear leaving home so she went back to Scotland. I can't remember the other girls' names. There was a big kitchen table; I used to eat with Mrs Sylvester in the dining room, just Patrick and me and if she was out I'd have it in the kitchen with them instead. The day nursery was down on the ground floor [basement], I didn't think much of that, anyone could have come down those steps in the middle of the night. Pat was about three I think, I can remember his curly hair and little sailor's suit. I stayed with him until he went to school."

Janet's routine meant that after breakfast each day they were off to the park until lunchtime and then again in the afternoon. "I used to go through the garden, straight from our place, over the high road near Barkers Department Store and all the Chinese, all yap, yap, yap, were on these seats with their little charges." Once sheltering from the rain she nipped into Barker's. "But although I didn't see Madam I got told off. 'I wish you wouldn't go in there but keep in the park'. I nearly put my notice in, but I thought, 'No, Janet, don't, nowhere else to go.' I earnt about £1 week I think, with my keep all in." At the end of the afternoon she played with her charge or read to him, and from the time he was in bed at 6 o'clock she stayed in the nursery, not going out in the evening. "Yes, I had one holiday but I didn't go home. I spent it with my friends in London. They were friends that came from Norfolk and were doing the same sort of thing. Yes, Diana H. and Mary Sale, she came from Martham. So I had an exciting time really. My two friends and I used to have Sundays off and Mother used to say if you get lost ask a policeman. So of course we had some cheap tickets to the zoo, went and saw everything that we wanted to see and we were coming home and we had had a cup of tea in a little shop and then we got lost and we didn't know where we were. So we went up to a policeman, he was on night duty…" and as Janet related the conversation with the policeman of all those years ago, she was reliving that day beside the Serpentine with her friends.

"My friends both came home, so London wasn't for me anymore and I came home on my own and got a job with the Watts at Hedley House in Carlton Colville. I lived in there but I didn't like Mr Watts; now he was brother to Rev. Hulver's wife at Ringsfield Rectory. My job there was just with the baby, 6 weeks old. I used to bathe the baby and Mrs Watts, she didn't know anything about babies and she used to come and watch me and I was so nervous I used to be glad when she had gone. The baby had a room of her own, which was normal, but I was on call during the night in case the children were ill, and I couldn't hear her so they changed the rooms and we went into the large bedroom so she was with me. Our meals were sent upstairs, we didn't eat with the servants, and Lucy, the maid, she now lives at Worlingham, she was the kitchen maid. I used to put the pram out in the rose garden and I remember once I could hear the hounds all coming out from Carlton Colville round by the church, well I ran and got the pram in and put it in the hall. Well, Mr Watts he came, 'Where's Elizabeth, where's Elizabeth? Oh, I was worried stiff, I knew the hounds were about.'"

Janet worked for a number of families. "There were very nice people, and if you got ladies and gentlemen they treated you as such but if you got somebody just made up, you know – I kept shy of them. I went temporary to the C's at Barsham; have you ever heard of them? Oh, he was a horrible man, very strict, he was a foreigner, Spanish or something. There were three children when I was there, only temporary whilst the nurse had a rest, as she (Mrs C) was expecting another baby. She was nice but he wasn't. He used to breed horses. Then there were the Dolbys at Lowestoft. Commander Mac, he was on HMS *Godetia*, I was there whilst they were at Lowestoft, 9, Gunton Cliff, right on the parade, right near to a millionaire, their sitting room looked right into our nursery. The family moved away. I didn't go with them, the parlour maid went but didn't stay away, long enough to just get them settled in. I usually looked after the children until they started school. I got attached to children so it was difficult to move on but some children you couldn't like."

The uniforms worn by children's nurses in those days were quite standard: a grey frock with stiff collars and cuffs and white aprons and caps, with a hat to be worn out of doors. In the nursery there were open fires which the maid had to see to. "Then we had the airing cupboard when we couldn't get the nappies dry; if we were hard up they had pulleys in the kitchen and we put them up there, but the cook didn't like that." Obviously there were strict rules and territorial rights below stairs.

"I finished up at the White House, Mettingham, Mrs Hodson. The only children who keep in contact are the Hodsons, they were the last ones before I got married in 1939." The only time that Janet went on holiday with the family was with the Hodsons, when they went to Southwold with the two children and they had a beach hut on the Esplanade.

"Mrs Hodson, she was missing, she didn't come down, but, Grandpa, he came down, Mr Hodson he came, redecorated all the chalet out. Who was the other nursery down there? The Hodsons and the Adairs of Flixton Hall, they were very friendly and the nanny from there used to come down to tea and vice versa, we used to go and have tea with them and sometimes the nannies were asked. They moved away didn't they, what was there? Four boys, I think, and the one boy, Richard and my charge, they used to go to school together and dancing class, everything together. The dancing class, we were taken by the chauffeur, and there were some American children, they had two nannies come with the three children. Who else? Father had a big road works and the two Colemans used to come, little tiny girl and the son; and Major Barnes' children from Sotterley Hall, three daughters came and the second one was ginger-haired. They had to learn the step one week and the next week go round on their own; this one girl she got the wrong foot, and nanny, she said, 'Patricia, Patricia.' She got the step wrong, oh, she couldn't get a thing right, the second girl couldn't. The nanny used to get so cross, I can remember her now." These dancing lessons held in Loddon for five and six year olds, were an important part of their social training. "Yes, the last place I was at was the best, there were three maids; Doris and Lucy, she married the sign writer, she was the house maid, was my nursery maid. Her mother lived in Ditchingham and on her afternoon off she asked if we would like to go and see her mother and she gave us some sandwiches, and I'm sure the meat was off. I'll always remember her sandwiches."

Janet met her future husband when she dropped a glove, quite innocently she maintains, on the road when she took the children for a walk and he gave it to her on the way back. He worked on the roads, keeping the verges tidy for the Council. They married in 1939 and came to Redisham to live, where they had a bit of pasture, kept ponies and pigs and of course his garden too.

"The first baby boy arrived in 1940, I just got over it and had one after the other, those four boys. I never looked at the last one for ages, I did so want a little girl."

All the time that Janet worked as a nursery nurse she didn't play the organ but when she moved to Redisham her skills were called upon again. At St. Peter's they were in need of a regular organist. A woman from the nearby market town used to come occasionally. "So my friend, Mrs Allard, she used to be in the same parish as me at Runham and she said, 'Janet used to play' so she let me in for it. Been playing the organ here for on and off 47 years, not all the time. Peter's [the church warden] mother was one that used to play, she used to make mistakes and Reverend Verrells, he used to say, 'MAUD! You're wrong, MAUD!' and she kept on going, she didn't pay any attention."

11

IN CONVERSATION WITH GEORGE & PHYLLIS

A FARMING LIFE

The residents in the nearby market towns called it Indian country, 'Indian' as in the wild west, because once ventured into it is not so easy to find one's bearings and find the way home. This is an area of nine parishes, covering less than 24 square miles, divided by a Roman road and offering a landscape of farmland and commons all dotted with numerous churches, most of which have registers dating back to the early sixteenth century. The farms boast names such as Shoe Devil and Sternacre (once Starve Acre, or even Stark Naked), but most of the farmhouses have been sold and stand independent of the land. City dwellers, with their urban sophistication, have moved in, not quite believing their luck when the sale of their town houses enabled them to buy the house of their dreams with a good-sized garden all in a perfect rural setting. They come not always with an understanding of the few quiet resident farmers and of those whom they call, not unkindly, the local peasants with their native knowledge.

Pubs have been converted into desirable dwellings as have the village shops. Most parish churches remain open, but their congregations have sadly dwindled, leaving the few to struggle on in an attempt to maintain these historic buildings, many of which have relics dating back to the Saxon and Norman periods.

How different it all was when George was born into a farming family in one of these parishes in 1908. The ownership of the land was mainly divided between a few major landowners including the Lord of the Manor and the Duke of Norfolk; there were, too, many small independent farmers most of whom rented the land, so that the total acreage was worked by around 161 farmers. These parishes were busy rural economies, each of which had a Public House, the Hawk, the Red Lion and the Jolly Farmers to name a few, the place to meet, have a mardle and relax with a pint. Many villages had blacksmiths and wheelrights, the occasional vetinary surgeon and, of course, a miller. Most had their own elementary school. It was such a different world to the one known today. If George could see it now, superficially much of the landscape would look familiar, although sadly with far fewer hedgerows. However he would look in vain for the mainly agricultural community; numerous farm workers are no longer needed; mammoth computerised machines have taken over. Strangely, the population has increased, council houses were built, more privately owned houses too and here and there the occasional and discreet industrial estate.

He is a tall man, slim and barely bowed for all his 94 years; quiet and slightly reticent. She, shorter and a little stouter and every inch the farmer's wife – practical, capable and direct. His farming ancestors came from Yoxford, some 15–20 miles away and had settled in St. Peter's in the late 19th century; hers, farmers too, from one of these nine parishes. George quickly recalls the farm he grew up on, the lanes, the beck and the land; they are almost part of his D.N.A. When it came to education there was a council elementary school in the next parish with between forty and fifty chidren. He takes up his story. "It was a small school. Mrs Scarwood was the teacher [she had taken over from one with the marvellous name of Miss Bertha Bloor], the building is still there but they use it for the village hall now. Then I was sent to Flixton where there was a master, rather than a school mistress, who they thought I needed. My friend from the next farm and I both went to Flixton, we biked there four or five miles. Then I went to Bungay Grammar [another five mile bicycle ride] there was a boys' school and a girls' school side by side. Parents paid in those days." The school was well established with a small number of pupils who enjoyed the facilities of an excellent school room and a science laboratory.

"I didn't go there long. I left when I was fifteen because my Father was taken ill and I had to do most of the work on the farm. I'd always helped on the farm. Didn't think of doing anything else. We were crazy to do it then, want to be doin' it. It was a small farm, only 50 acres. It was not all arable, some pasture, about six cows and two horses. No, there wasn't any electricity. We had a candle lantern fust, you cleaned the glass and then stuck the candle in the little ol' thing in the middle of the lantern and lit it. But weren't that a gentle light. We still go to one church for Harvest Festival and it's all candles, it's lovely. Then we got our paraffin lantern. You used to carry them about in the yard, the flame used to blow about, but it didn't go out."

Folklore tells us that the Archangel St. Michael, to put it bluntly, kicked the Devil out of heaven. The Devil landed in a bramble bush, and being none too happy he cursed it and spat on it, so that for generations it was held that you never pick blackberries after St. Michael's Day which is Michaelmas. This tale and Michaelmas weather warnings, such as 'If Michaelmas brings many acorns Christmas will cover the ground with snow' were all remembered amongst the country folk. How relevant such weather forcasting would be now with our changing weather patterns who knows. Michaelmas, the 29th September, the end of the harvest season, had for hundreds of years important significance amongst the farming community and not just for old tales that were told. This was the time when houses and land changed hands and farm hands and domestic servants were hired for the coming year. Goose Fairs and Sheep Sales were held, all signifying that the harvest was over and it was now a time for much activity and change. However it seemed that not many farms changed hands at Michaelmas in these nine parishes.

"I think they stuck longer in a place than they do now. They rented the farms then, most of them around there were on the Flixton Estate. In 1921 all the little farms and the worst ones were sold off, and they just kept a few on the Estate. Father bought ours in '21 but those that rented had a secure tenancy, paying their rent twice a year. If you were a poor farmer they turned you out."

Whilst her future husband had a secure childhood, early life for Phyllis had not been so easy. She too came from farming stock, however she was to be denied a childhood spent with her parents and siblings. "I worked at home with my grandmother until I was fifteen. My mother was ill after she had me and I think they said she was in bed for two years. Well, I was taken from my mother when I was two days old and I was with my grandmother until she died. Then I went home. I always said I would never let a child of mine be brought up with a grandmother. I never accepted my mother." Eventually another girl was born and eleven years later three successive boys came along and it was obviously hard for Phyllis that she was not part of that family during her formative years. At the beginning the infant's grandparents were farming, as in the family tradition and then they took over a Public House.

"They were the best days of my childhood in there. There was a Mr Harold, he used to teach me the time and all sorts of things, that old gentleman used to. Then there were four brothers, the Hunters, they were characters. Moley, he had lost an arm in the Great War, he used to catch moles, he'd skin 'em and then sell the skins. One or two of them often used to go thatching corn stacks, helping farmers until haysel. When they had got a bit of money they would come into the pub and get drunk. Once they'd got a little money that's what they done and they'd stop there a week. When grandmother took over the Jolly Farmers one of the brothers used to go there and stop for at least a week. My grandmother used to feel sorry for him, yet he was a bloomin' nuisance. He'd lay in the barn and she would take him some bread and cheese or something of whatever she had and then he'd come back in the pub when it was opening time and have another do before going back to sleep in the barn. That was Harry Hunter, they called him Fudge. They were good workers when they did work, you always saw that, but they liked a holiday!"

So in this sparsely populated rural area how did our couple meet? He laughs, "I don't know, I think Mother [not once did he refer to her by her Christian name] think Mother was out for a walk on the road and I was biking past." Phyllis joins in, "Just talked and then it added on. Now we've been married nearly 69 years. We've had our ups and downs, but there you are."

They were courting for around two years and then married in1934. Up until then after George's mother had died he had had a live-in housekeeper. Phyllis takes up the story, "Mrs Lovuck, a great, huge woman weren't she? When he was milking and bringing the milk in she would stand in the passage right in the way. Anyway we married in 1934, went to work the next morning. There weren't many people went on honeymoon, not farmers anyhow. We've done more travelling in our later life than we've done any time. We had to wait till the oldest boy was 22 yrs. when we first went away, we never had a holiday till then."

George had gradually taken over the running of the farm from his father. "When I first took over I kept more cows and started selling milk. See my mother made butter; they drove down to Bungay in a pony cart and she had one grocer that took butter off her. We had to have cows to get a living. We grew wheat and barley and the root crops for the cows."

Although a new wife, the working life for Phyllis was the same as she had always been accustomed to. "We had a pump over the sink, the water came from what they used to call the Tea Pond. That used to come up a drain to a well outside the back door, that was supposed to be clean then! You used to draw water out of the well with a pump. We were used to it; wherever you went everyone was doing the same thing. That was manual work then. The Horse Pond and another one for the house, the Tea Pond. For hot water there was an old copper; then you used to have the bath by the fire and bring the water to the bath. We had a cellar and marble shelves, you make a jelly or anything and that's where you put it. I knew nothing else. I hardly ever use the fridge for anything now because I don't like it. I never looked out onto bricks and mortar, that was hard when we come here."

When the couple had finally retired from farming, leaving it to the next generation, they had 'sensibly' moved into the nearby market town, and it must have been very hard as all their lives up until then had been lived in the heart of the country. How do you adapt to town life after over seventy years of knowing nothing else around you but fields and trees and your nearest neighbour out of sight? She admitted also that she had difficulty making conversation with her present neighbours, friendly though they were, as all she had known was farming.

She continues, "We never went into each other's houses because we hadn't the time. I mean, when I had the boys at home I used to bake fourteen loaves of bread a week. I used to do all my own baking. Used to go into town just once a week and we used to get a ten stone sack of flour at a time. Tuesday and Fridays I used to bake. Once we moved to Brook Hall I had an Esse, it was a big cream thing with four ovens. An Esse, they were good old stoves, you used to have them with coals. We used to make them up at night and we used to make a beeline for the kitchen 'cause it never went out. If you did let it go out you started it with Phurnacite, it was a smokeless coal for stoves, little shiny nobbles. I used to cook the meat in one oven, cakes in another and pastry in another. My daughter-in-law, she had one of those ovens in the wall, a brick oven, it went back miles in the wall, that kept red hot and you just made things and stuck 'em all in. The trouble was she had no controls but I did with the Esse, because the thing where the fire was you could turn it off the oven, straight up, or on the oven, three heats.

"We had breeder sows at different times. I used to fatten one up especially for the house. Sell the fat pigs, but keep this one. We used to kill our own pig at St. Peter's, then later on we would take it down to the slaughter house, used to take it down to Lambert's in Earsham in them days. Anyway, we used to pickle it. You had a great big tub and with this coarse salt in and all sorts you used to make a brine. You cut the pig up and what went in there became ham and salt pork. If you didn't want it all in then you just left parts out. You used to pickle it in there for some time, then you used to take it out and take it to somebody with a smoke house; great sides, hang 'em up they did in this smoke house, and then we used to hang 'em up at home when they come back. That bacon used to be beautiful. It took me a week to make pork cheese and lard. The last pig we had killed I made 45lb lard. Oh, that was beautiful, that made lovely short cakes." Nodding at her husband, "He won't eat a bought cake."

For beef they went to the butcher. Their own cattle were sold at Norwich or Ipswich Market, very occasionally at Beccles. As ever it was the farmer's wife who was in charge of the poultry, so they had a chicken on the table when they wanted one and their own eggs, the majority of which were collected by a firm from Loddon, Carters. The garden provided the vegetables and usually one of the children was dispatched to pick the vegetables for lunch. "You can't beat going out and getting your own." We can all agree with that.

In the parish of St.Peter's where George was farming he recalled there being just two fair-sized farms and three small ones. The blacksmith was in the next village. "That's where we used to go to have the horses shod; and he used to shoe the wheels, put the rims on. They were wooden wheels and they used to heat the iron rim and hammer it on. In the summer time these wheels would shrink, dry weather and the wheels got loose and wobbly, so you had to take them to the blacksmith and he'd tighten this iron rim up, put a peg in the middle and pull the woodwork together, felloes they called them, and they would draw them up and tighten this iron rim till it was tight again.

"The mill? That was in the next parish at St. Michael's too. We would take our corn there to grind for the cattle. Eventually we bought our own little mill with an oil engine in the barn, mainly for the corn and we would grind up oats and beans for the cattle too. We sold the wheat and barley, we used to go into the Bungay King's Head and Charlie Marsden was going then. He used to buy most of the wheat round here for flour for Earsham Mill; he bought a lot of the wheat roundabouts. We used to cut it with a self binder, we'd stack it and thrash it. He'd have a sample he'd look at it, smell it and such like and he'd bid you for it. There were none of these 'ere tests or whatever in them days, they'd just look at it, especially barley, they'd smell it for the malt."

"We used a little top dressing of sulphate of ammonia on the land but other than that we just had farm yard manure. We put it in a heap all during the winter and after harvest you cart it out onto the stubble and spread it. It had rotted down alright. There were no sprays about then. If we had 10 coombs an acre that was a good crop, that's 200cwt of barley and just under for wheat; wheat was 18 stone a coomb, barley was 16. It's hundredweights and tons now, it was coombs then. Four year rotation, they don't do that now."

"Something will come unstuck one day," Phyllis chipped in.

"They can grow it now, year after year; well, we couldn't then, not very well. We'd grow beans and the wheat behind that, beans and clover [clover hay], barley behind the roots, mangolds and whatever. Never had a problem selling, you had to take what they offered you; the prices are set now. I used to have someone chance time to help chop out the beet and all that sort of thing, but I did all the hedging and ditching myself. I enjoyed it. Everybody was doing it, all the farmers around were doing the same as we were doing, so you just took it as that's what happened. You didn't look to sit on your backside, did you?

"We used to brew beer for harvest with a bushel of malt. I used to work in with my next door neighbour, we used to harvest together. We didn't have a harvest supper so we had the beer which they used to drink as they went. There were a lot of men so we had one of those big brown bottles in the harvest field. My grandfather used to take a gallon of beer into the field at breakfast time. We used to buy a bushel of malt from the corn merchant in Bungay, malt and hops. Put it in a cask and work it. You have to scald this malt with hot water, put that on and let it stand all night, then drain the beer from the hops and malt and that was that. Put it in the cask, put a little yeast in, and that would work for a day or two and you would have root, or rude beer. That would be stronger than what you buy now."

When it came to thrashing, then machinery would be brought in and the refreshment for this very dry and thirsty work was different. "Thrashing, yes them old steam engines, they used to do that all winter. We used to stack the corn and then they used to come round and thrash the stacks out. They'd come within a little when you wanted them. Yes, they had a whole winter's work thrashing. The chap we had, Collier from St.Margaret, he got so he had five or six tackles going round. Then when the steam engines went out he had those Field Marshall Tractors.

"We used to make cider then, some men used to take a day or two off and come and help with the thrash; well I don't know how Ted liked it when they were missing from his farm. We used to give the thrashing people cider to drink, that was a little too much for some of them. That got a hold of them sometimes. When we had finished thrashing we always cut a certain amount of barley straws up for chaff they called it. They got so they couldn't bag this chaff off the chaff cutter, so they had to run it onto the floor, and were scrabbing it in with their hands into the bags. We had someone from Bungay, well he swore at them. A man come round with his old van and a press. Any apples, whatever you had got; we had an orchard at St. Peter's, we'd get up them ladders and shake them off the trees. This man, he would grind the apples up and then press them and you just had the juice. Square box and all mats, they'd put a mat in, coconut matting, and then a layer of pulp, then another mat and more pulp, seven or eight mats I suppose; then they'd screw the top of the press and press 'em down and squeeze the juice out the bottom. Then you had the juice and you fed it with sugar and apple cider. You knew you'd got cider, it's not like the stuff in a bottle now. Kept it in a casket; didn't leave it very long after you had fed it a time or two. The older it got the stronger it got. You could drink it, but my goodness me the top of your head come off if you had a drop too much. You could put rump steak into the cask of that cider and that would eat it up, that was good stuff, but that had a delayed reaction."

Today the County Agricultural Shows are big affairs. They not only showcase every aspect of farming, be it livestock or machinery, but they have country crafts and clothing and many, many other things on sale. The flower tent, which assaults all the senses with its beautiful blooms, colours and heady perfume, is always amongst one of the most popular places to visit, almost as attractive a draw as the W.I. Tent and their cooking, which is another regular port of call. People have a day off work, as do children from school, to go and enjoy the events in the grand arena, with not just livestock vying for a rosette and an enormous rise in their stud value, but show-jumping, motor cycle and parachuting displays. These shows, which since the 1950s have had a permanent site in both Suffolk and Norfolk, are now big business, but in their present form they are comparatively modern. Initially they were much smaller affairs and purely agricultural. In Suffolk it all started in 1831 when a group of farmers and landowners met at the White Hart in Wickham Market with the thought of organising an agricultrual show. The idea was that such an event would give farmers the opportunity to meet, to discuss new innovations and to bring their prize bull or heavy horse, and any other livestock to compete in front of their peers. As a consequence of this meeting of minds the East Suffolk Agricultural Association was formed as a charity and the Earl of Stradbroke was to be its first President. The first show was held on 21st September 1832. One year later, West Suffolk followed suit until twenty years on they merged. Originally the shows were held at different venues and various Market towns; Stowmarket, Saxmundham, Wickham Market, and of course Beccles, Framlingham and Sudbury were amongst those who played host to these events. As they grew increasingly popular the large towns of Ipswich and Bury St. Edmund's were a greater attraction.

George remembers, "There was one here at Beccles, one at Halesworth and one on Bungay Common. That was when the Beccles show was on those meadows on the corner out to Ringsfield that I bought my first tractor in 1937. A Standard Fordson, that cost £100 brand new and a little furrow Ransome plough. Those days you didn't sort of finish the work up with a tractor, nowadays they go from one hedge to another, that's a double furrow plough. Well, in those days it was only a single plough, so you only ploughed one way like you did with the horses, up one side and down the other, so you didn't finish the work up with the tractor, you finished up with horses, the last two furrows sort of thing. You didn't run the tractor on the ploughed land to finish them off. We did afterwards, we didn't worry so much. Tractors had iron wheels and a spud wheel, a round iron wheel with all spuds on, and then they got so they made iron wheels for them different patterns. Mostly Ransomes and Ford made tractors for what we had and they were Ransome spud wheels.

"You did miss working with horses after a time, but it was a lot easier and you soon got used to that. Horses knew what you said when they worked with you. Some of the old ones they knew each other, horses and horsemen. An old man, he was a horseman for my grandfather, one time that he was working he took a load of malt and barley down to Halesworth. He come home by Wisset Plough, stopped to have a drink or two and he made a bet that he could drive his horses home with no reins and he did. From Wisset Plough round those country lanes to St. Lawrence Grove he just talked to them and they knew exactly what he meant. Well, there wasn't anything on the roads in those days. You see they took interest in what they were doing then. My grandfather, he didn't do a lot of work, not at St.Lawrence Grove, and he went out and came home one night a bit boozy. He didn't get up very soon in the morning and the old man went underneath the window and he say,

'Where are we going to drill today Master?'

He say, 'Finish that field you are in.'

'I've done that.'

'How do you do that?

He said, 'Trotted up and down the field, and galloped round the ends.'

"Twelve acres, he thought that was a lot then."

Tractors came into their own but George's love of horses persisited and he started to breed Suffolk Punches, the traditional plough horse. This breed was developed for farm work because it was both powerful and docile and generally lived a long healthy life. The early twentieth century saw it increase in popularity and because they were rarely sold the bloodline was kept pure. To be able to register a horse in the Suffolk Punch Stud Book, which was the official register of the pedigree horses, a new foal had to have had both sire and dam entered in the pedigree register. It was with obvious pride when George said, "I had a horse in the book once. Mayflower." Many thousand were registered at the time of the first war. By the second world war mechanisation had taken its toll and just 6,000 were registered; by 1966 the number was down to a worrying nine. Today the number has crept up to around 500 as individuals and organisations work to save this very beautiful breed.

As these parishes were known for their various commons it was quite normal, even until recent times, for some gypsies to establish themselves there. In those days they were the genuine

article, on the whole courteous and hard working. As one of the older gypsies recently said, 'You can go anywhere in this world with soap and water and a civil tongue.'

"Gypsies? Yes, they weren't no trouble. In our parish in St. Peter's they used to pull up on the grass at the side of the road for the night, or a little while. They'd stop a week sometimes, and sold the pegs and lace and things, but there was not much seasonal work for them. They nearly all had a good dog, a long dog, and they used to go poaching at night for hares and things I suppose. We had very little game on our place, but you wouldn't worry about a rabbit."

The response came back with lightning speed when asked if there had been a local poacher: "Yes, in Bungay. Ralph, he lived down Bridge Street. He wrote a book *I Walked By Night*, and he did too. He used to poach a lot, and he had a boy to do the same. He worked for me for a little while and he told me once he was at Ditchingham Hall, he was on the other side of the moat; whether the gamekeepers chased after him or not I don't know, but he put the gun in his mouth and swam across the moat."

As a boy George had gone out with a long stick with a spoon tied on the end for waterhen's eggs. Their family of country children followed in his footsteps, going up the becks with their spoon on a stick and bringing the eggs home for their mother to fry for their breakfast – "Oooh, they were good!" The girls competed with the boys, always trying to keep up. "Three times Joy nearly drowned. She went across the bridge over the beck when that was full and there was ice on the bridge and fell in; they pulled her out. Then there used to be a big, tall tank in the shed full of water to cool the milk. Course she'd got to get up on the top haven't she and got to look in. In she go, her sister got her out then. I forget where else she went, she had three lots of water, come home soaked. The times I took her down the doctor's with either a pencil or a stone up her nose, she wasn't satisfied until she'd got something up her nose. She was one weren't she?"

Fond family memories, but another more serious occasion was vividly recalled, and this goes back to wartime. Their farm at St. Peter's was close to the new Flixton airfield, barely three miles from the village itself. In the early years of the war the village was the Bungay police collection point for the Home Guard to bring any airmen, British or German, who had bailed out of their aircraft so they were accustomed to seeing members of the forces around, but their quiet rural life was rarely disturbed. By 1942, however, Flixton was chosen as one of the many sites for the American Air Force in East Anglia. A new airfield was built with three runways and dispersal pads for the aircraft to stand on, hangars for maintenance, a hospital and living quarters for over 2,000 men. Such an influx was quite a shock for a village with a population of less than 150 and the constant waves of planes coming and going were something quite new. It was 1944 and the Liberators were returning. Phyllis takes up the story. "February, about four in the morning I used to pull the blinds and would say, 'Begger Jerry'. They were blackouts and I got fed up. And then I said to him, 'I don't know I can hear something crackling somewhere, something.' I knew all these planes were coming in 'cause we were in the drome, in the ring, inside the lights.

They had a ring of lights, two mile right round the drome and we were inside that. I woke him up and said, 'There's something wrong here somewhere.' When I took the curtains and the blackouts down the straw was coming past the bloomin' window, all alight. We had a thatched house with new netting and the incendary bombs were catching in the netting. I looked out of our window and the stack was going up; I said, 'We're on fire!' I had two older children, we woke them up. Poor little devils didn't know where they were goin'. I said, 'You'll have to come out, put on whatever you can,' and I let them put on whatever they could, one had a rubber boot and one had a shoe. Anyway, the babe was near our bed. I got the two up and down the stairs, and then I went for her. I couldn't see in the room, I couldn't, that was full of smoke before that burst into flame, 'cause it was, what do you call it, lath and plaster, wooden-framed house, a real old farmhouse. Anyway, poor little 'ol' girl was crying her eyes out, I got her out by the hair of her head because I couldn't see and wrapped her in this blanket and laid her in a chair downstairs while I put some clothes on. I was half dressed, but I couldn't get back to get anything. The Red Cross and the Bungay doctor were good to us afterwards because everything went up. We had clothes coupons then. The flaming straw was dropping down near the doors, they couldn't get anything out. We lost everything, they got two leather chairs out, but the flames were so fierce that they scorched them even though they had set them right down the bottom of the garden. I think the fire brigade came when it was nearly over; that was burning all along Lowestoft and all that, they really set about us, but there you go. The aerodrome lights came on when they were coming in, the Jerries come with them, they mixed themselves in with all the American planes, they were shooting the Yanks down as they were landing. There were 24 boys went down on the marshes. That got so that the Americans at Flixton they would not go out at night as they had so many shot down, only daytime; so it was our boys, the RAF, who went at night."

A cottage was found on the estate for the family and farming went on as usual. The supply of the nation's food was essential. In the vicinity some farmers had Italian P.O.W.s working for them.

"I didn't, didn't need any. You had Land Girls when you thrashed, they used to travel with the thrashing machine. Everything was rationed, feed for the cattle, everything. You'd got to plant all the land and you'd got to farm it up to a standard or they would take it away from you."

Farming, which had been in the doldrums before the war, now had a revival which continued after the war for some time as the country and the rest of Europe struggled to recover. George and Phyllis' burnt-out farmhouse was eventually rebuilt although it took two years. But when they were able to move back they found that times had changed. Instead of the pump from the Tea Pond they had running water and now no more candles or paraffin lanterns. Poles were going up and it wasn't long before they had electricity too. In the post-war period the heavy horses were increasingly less likely to be seen working the land; tractors were the norm and they were becoming more versatile. Although combines were used on some farms in the 1930s, now the characteristic red of the Massey Harris combine harvester, originally fuelled by TVO (Tractor Vapourising Oil) stood out in the landscape. And the threshing tackles had had their day. The 1947 Agricultural Act guaranteed prices amongst other things in an attempt to guarantee the security of the nation's food supply. Farmers have, sometimes grudgingly, had to adapt to many changes over the years, but perhaps not such drastic change as George witnessed from his early working days to his retirement. Certainly the mechanisation made life easier but also lonelier and hard work had never been an issue, but he also witnessed more and more bureaucratic interference, more paper work and regulations. Which life would he have preferred?

12

JOHN

COURTEOUS BEYOND ALL ELSE

The gathering was a lunch to celebrate his ninetieth birthday. There must have been close on sixty or seventy people there, relatives, friends of long standing and those of us who had known John only a mere twenty or thirty years. His speech was very short and with great humility he thanked everyone for coming, thanked them for their friendship and very movingly said how fortunate he felt himself to be. It was a room full of love and genuine affection for a man who had lived a long and full life. There was nothing very distinguished about John, a small man with a round face, spectacles, thinning hair, always tidily dressed in sports jacket and tie. Yet his gentle voice, which would lapse into Suffolk dialect for the sheer fun of it, and above all his natural courtesy made an instant impression of his being a gentleman in the truest sense of the word.

In 1880 the *Ipswich Journal* reported 186 Ramsgate boats trawling out of Lowestoft. The fishing industry in Lowestoft was growing rapidly as was the population of the town when the families from Ramsgate followed their menfolk and settled there. Amongst these families were the Ratcliffes, George and

Walter, who owned a number of fishing vessels; they moved into Lowestoft's Clapham Road amongst the town's own fishing families. Perhaps it was inevitable that two local fishermen, Percy and Walter, married Walter Ratcliffe's daughters, Ethel and Eliza, and no doubt more marriages followed. It was into this fishing community of joint Suffolk and Kentish heritage that our John, celebrating his 90th birthday in 2013, was born.

Fishing in Lowestoft dates back to the Middle Ages when superstition led the fishermen to believe that because the sun rose there before anywhere else in England it brought good luck and good catches! From the end of the 18th century a Beach Village grew up along the bottom of the cliff at the most easterly point, virtually becoming a town in its own right, with pubs, shops, schools and churches and even its own brewery and abattoir. However it was one man in particular who helped turn the town into a major fishing port – Sir Morton Peto, who in 1847 bought Lowestoft harbour and then introduced the railway into the town, enabling him to proudly boast that freshly caught fish in Lowestoft would be on the tea tables in Manchester that same day. It has always been the case that many neighbouring villages and towns are in normally 'friendly' competiton with each other. Such was the competition between the two ports of Lowestoft and Great Yarmouth. For years Great Yarmouth with the larger fleet had the advantage and was known as the herring capital of the world. Peto's new harbour and railway gave Lowestoft a boost but then came the great revolution – steam. Until the end of the 1890's all fishing had been done under sail and so the fishermen were particularly dependant on the vagaries of the weather. A steam drifter, the English prototype, was built and launched in Lowestoft in 1897. In appearance 'The Consolation of Lowestoft' was simply a sailing smack with a funnel; she still had two masts, a full sailing rig and was steered by a tiller; below deck, however, was a boiler and a little two cylinder steam engine. So successful was this venture that by 1903 Lowestoft had over 300 steam drifters registered; by now they were fitted with a wheelhouse and a steering wheel. No longer were drifters prevented from unloading their catch by lack of wind delaying their homeward trip. Steam drifters were so successful that they created a boom period in the shipyards. Despite the cost of between £3,000 and £4,000 per ship more and more fishermen invested in them. Consequently the fishing industry expanded and herring catches grew year by year. The bonanza year came in 1913 when 1,360,400 crans of herring were landed at Lowestoft and Great Yarmouth. Sadly 'The Consolation of Lowestoft', the vessel which instigated this boom, was destroyed by fire in Lerwick in 1907.

It was in this era of growth in the latter half of the 19th century that John's grandfather started work. "My grandfather was a fish salesman. I must tell you about him because he was a gentleman I had tremendous regard for. He started life at 8 yrs. old selling fish in the streets of Lowestoft and at 11 yrs. old he went to sea as a ship's boy. Eventually he bought his own ship, a smack, then he built up a fleet. [His vessels formed an impressive list which may have included 'LT454 Young Percy' and 'LT455 Young Bert', named after his two sons.] He was a very hard working gentleman, a very generous man and as I say I had tremendous admiration for him because he did it all by sheer guts and he was kind with it. So, that was grandfather. Well, my father worked with him in the same business. [It would have been a proud day when '& Son' was added to the firm's name.] No, he didn't go to sea, he was a fish salesman in Lowestoft. Eventually, when grandfather died, we moved to a house on Gunton Cliff at Lowestoft, which was lovely and then the war came along and my father and mother moved to Fleetwood temporarily because that's where the fishing fleet moved to during the war, and he died in 1944 which was very sad because, again, I had tremendous admiration for my

Father. I think he was the nicest man I ever knew. Sorry, but that was just the way it was." John was touchingly and quietly embarrassed about admitting his feelings for his Father.

Following the record catches of 1913, the outbreak of war the next year had a devastating effect on the fleet. Many steam drifters and trawlers were commandeered and many fishermen joined the royal navy or, if they were too old, the Royal Naval Reserve. The fishermen and their families in the Beach Village were particularly vulnerable to bombardment, and the risks from German submarines for those still fishing were immense whilst the number of herring caught plummeted compared to the previous year. However the one good thing that resulted from the first war was that the fish stocks had the opportunity to recover from what had been considerable over-fishing, just as wildlife in the rural areas had a respite from the amount of hunting and particularly the shooting of birds for their feathers that had been fashionable at the time.

As with so many of his generation John was born into a very different world from the one we know today. A Suffolk man through and through, he was born in Lowestoft in 1923. It was not long before the family moved further up the road to live with his grandfather who was alone following the death of his wife and in John's words "It was a lovely house." From selling fish in the street at the age of eight his grandfather had become a very affluent man.

We seemed to have raced through the first twenty years of John's youth, so to return to the 1920's and the beginning of his education. "My first school, St. Margaret's College, was a private school in the house of the Headmaster who was called Tungate. I already knew him as a member of the church which I atttended. I should think there were about 25 young boys and strangely enough quite a lot of the boys in Lowestoft who made their way in the world started there. I look back with quite happy thoughts of those chaps I met there. It was just a school for the 3 'R's, we used dots for counting and that sort of thing, it was good, it went very well." Towards the end of his time there, when he was around ten years old... "It was a day in January and I had some friends who lived just along the road and we were walking along the north beach at Lowestoft with Mrs S., their mother. These two boys and I walked out to the end of the groyne and I fell in. And I had reason to be thankful because Mrs S., wearing a fur coat and gold watch, came in and fished me out. There is no doubt about it, if it hadn't been for her I shouldn't be here; that is quite remarkable.

"Then I moved to the Grammar School. There was an entrance exam. It was a very good school and I was very happy there. The teachers were all good and I was involved in the amateur dramatic society and also the school choir. We used to do an annual play and we performed at speech days and things. The music master was Ernest Rymer and the classics and English master, Baker, they used to get together and write a school musical play, not opera, which was very good and that was one thing I appeared in." [John had been having singing lessons for some time and his love of music was fostered at home.] "My Father was musical, he played the piano and organ and he was also the Sunday School Superintendent in the church. He used to turn out on Sunday mornings and again in the afternoon and we all used to go to all the services in the morning and evening. He played and my Mother, she liked music, she sang and as I said I had singing lessons. Then I went onto the piano and my Father said that if I got a good grade in the school certificate I could learn the organ. Well, I got a sufficiently good result. I really wanted that because I had always wanted to play the organ; for some reason that was a special instrument for me. So I went to St. Margaret's Church for lessons and the teacher was the organist there, Cyril Mitchell. He was a great man with a tremendous sense of humour. He knew that I was passionately fond of motor cars and he used to compare playing the organ to driving the motor car saying, 'You must be comfortable, you must know where all the controls are.' He was a great chap, he died twenty or thrirty years ago."

Music played a large part throughout John's life, however whilst at school that other life-long passion developed – cars.

"Oh, crummy, it was a boy's interest to start with. I used to take the *Motor Magazine* as a boy and we had had a car ever since I could remember. In 1925 my father had a big Rover Tourer and then I can remember going with him and my brother to the Norwich Motor Company when we bought a Singer 12 saloon which was like a big house on wheels. Every year we used to go and stay with an aunt of my father's, Aunt Totty, in Lexton which was at the south end of Colchester. So we all piled into the car. In those days you had a luggage grid on the back; about six cases were piled up and off we used to go. Eventually the Singer went and we had a Morris 10 and then a Morris 12. I had a school friend, Cyril Rist. He was my mate and we both had a great interest in motor cars and motor bikes. We lived on Gunton Cliff, the north end of Lowestoft, and Cyril lived in Oulton Broad and we used to meet every Saturday. I used to cycle over to him, then home for lunch and back again to Oulton Broad in the afternoon, about three or four miles each way. It kept me fit. So from the tender age of twelve we had a motor bike between us. We used to work on this bike in his garage and his Father was associated with a firm in Lowestoft which had a large playing field which we used to ride round on our bike. We had about six bikes over the years; the very first one we had strangely enough was a 1917 motorcycle. It really was a museum piece."

It wasn't until the beginning of the 20th century that motorbikes started to be produced commercially so John and Cyrils's first bike really must have been rather special.

"Then we had a Douglas BSA and finished with a Morgan 3-wheeler which we only paid a couple of quid for. It was an interesting one, very old and had a wooden body, with typical Morgan chassis and works. We used to drive that round the field. Eventually that went to the breakers. The last vehicle that Cyril and I bought was a 1929 Austin Seven, we got it from a breakers yard for thirty shillings. This was all in the late 1930's and before I started work in 1938."

It wasn't until 1932 that Britain overtook the French when car production, which had virtually come to a standstill during the first World War, reached 379,310 passenger cars; traffic on the roads was not heavy and some horse-drawn vehicles were still to be seen.

"We had this Austin before I was old enough to have a licence. At that time my Father had that very nice Morris 12. We didn't keep it at ours because there was no garage and my Father used to have to take it to a garage in a road nearby but obviously he used to park it outside during the day. And, as Fathers do, he used to rest in a chair after lunch and he would leave the key in the car. One day when I was sixteen I took off in it and drove it up to the end of the road and along the sea wall and back. He never knew."

That feeling of part daring and part guilt still sat on John's shoulders seventy-four years later. However, as soon as his seventeenth birthday dawned it was time to make his driving official with a licence. The driving test was just a formality for someone who had had so much time behind the wheel already in his young life. "This was just a matter of driving round and doing a turn in the road, backing in, that sort of thing, going through the usual routine. The most important thing was the emergency stop. They asked a few questions, not anything like today. In those days the licence was a little red book; you sent it away and they used to stick a page in for renewal. Unfortunately they kept the original one but they did give me one back in 1940. Now, of course I get it for free.

"I was so enthusiastic that I wanted to go into the motor business but my Father wasn't very impressed, so I was happy to go into engineering instead. I left school at fifteen, nearly sixteen, and joined the Borough Engineer's Department in Lowestoft as a pupil to the Borough Engineer. There was no question of going into the family business; the fishing trade was gradually winding down and my Father never thought of suggesting that I should follow him, so that was alright. So I go down to Lowestoft Town Hall, the Borough Surveyor's Department, as a pupil. Being a pupil, I was put in the general office with two young ladies; one of them, Catherine, is still alive, she's been a widow for years; I periodically go and say hello. The other one was Betty. That's the day I met my darling wife. [John was just sixteen.] We got on very well, we both loved sailing; her parents had a sailing boat and I had one with her brother. So we did a lot of sailing on the Broads.

"Then the war came along, my parents followed the fishing fleet up to Fleetwood and I went to stay with a lady and her husband. She had been our maid." To John any woman was a 'lady', even the maid, to be treated by him with the respect due to her sex.

"My grandfather had two maids in his gorgeous house which had a longish lawn where we used to have bowls drives and the like and the church fête. At the beginning of the war the chemistry master, the stinks master we called him, became Gas Identification Officer for the local A.R.P. and I was working for the Borough Council and was also working on the rescue and so on and he came to see me and said, 'I'm the Gas Identification Officer and I want an assistant.' The only reason he wanted an assistant was that he knew I had a car. So I became the assistant GIO. From then on I used to go to breakers yards, so after the Austin which Cyril and I had, I bought a Morris 12 and the last one before I joined the army was a Fiat; it was a 12 horse power Fiat, dicky seat, lovely old car; it was £7 10s. As I was a GIO I got a special permit and didn't have to pay tax on it and I got a special petrol allowance. Anyway, back to wartime. I had a brother, Peter, he was two and a half years older than me and he was in the Territorials so that at the outbreak of war he went straight to France and that was the last we saw of him. Very sadly he was lost at Dunkirk. I can remember quite clearly the house we had on Gunton Cliff, it was requisitioned by the army and I used to go there periodically to collect mail and to see they weren't pulling the house down. On one occasion I went and there was a War office letter saying that my brother was missing presumed lost. That was the only thing we were ever told."

John must have had the upsetting task of relating this news to his parents in Fleetwood. How did they feel when their younger son felt, as a consequence of losing his brother, that he too should volunteer? "I didn't have to go because I was in a reserved occupation as a student, but I felt I ought to go. I still had the old Fiat so before I joined up I drove this old car up to Fleetwood to see my parents and to put it in a garage there. Eventually my Father wrote me a letter asking whether it was worth keeping the old car and paying for a garage for it. We decided that it wasn't and there was another fishing family up there who had a son with them and we gave it to him."

It was 1942 when aged nineteen he joined up as a Sapper and following his initial training went off to North Africa. "After about a year I was sent home to get a commission. On the troop ship travelling back to Liverpool, in the midst of the Atlantic, a chap came up to me, a sergeant who I didn't know.

'Do you have a brother Peter?'

'Yes.'

'Was he in the 58 Medium Regiment?'

'Well, I expect you know he was lost at Dunkirk?'

'Yes I do.'

'I was in the same unit and I saw him get on a ship, being evacuated, and the ship sank.'"

How did he feel learning this news out of the blue? Was it better to know what happened or did it add to the anguish? "That was the only information that we really had as to what happened to Peter. But, what an amazing thing wasn't it, miles away from anywhere. My youngest son took me over to Dunkirk and we went to see the memorial with all the names on but obviously no grave because he wasn't there to be buried.

"Having done my officer training I was posted to Preston and from there I got my second pip and I was posted to India, Lahore, where I got my third pip and became a Captain. A friend of mine and I were posted into the Royal Indian Army in their war headquarters. We both went to the HQ of the No.1 E.N.M. Battalion. We had two months of Indianisation when we were taught Urdu and learnt various bits and pieces about India. Then I was posted to the battle school which was at Bindraban Camp; it was right up in the north in the foothills of the Himalayas. One couldn't have asked for a better place in India; the climate was acceptable which was good. I was O.C. Battle School. What happened was the Indian sepoys, the Indian soldiers, came in from civilian life and invariably had to have months of ordinary civilian training, you know using knives and forks and that sort of thing, and then they had a military course. This was '44/'45 and as I say I was O.C. Battle School and I had two British officers and four hundred Indian troops. I was very lucky to be there rather than in a lot of worse places.

"Eventually I was demobbed and I came home. Sadly my Father had died in 1944, my Mother had bought a bungalow in Lowestoft and was living on her own so I went to live with her. In '42 when I went off to the army Betty and I had got engaged. A long engagement, we didn't get married until after the war when we married at the Methodist Church in the Hight Street in Lowestoft. It has since been demolished. So as I say, I came back to live with Mother, my Father had died, my brother was killed, my cousin Bernard, who was in the R.A.F., was killed. I came back when the war finished in '45/'46 and we got married in '47. I went straight back to the Council, my tutelage was finished and they gave me a job as an engineering assistant. The chief assistant, Ronnie Downes, who was a very nice chap, had worked with the famous S.W. Mobbs."

Mobbs was an authority on sea defence. He was the man who designed and built the sea wall at Lowestoft and he also used to sub-contract himself to local authorities along the Norfolk coast as consultant. "Eventually Sidney Mobbs became Chief Engineer of the Norfolk and Suffolk River Authortiy and he got in touch with Ronnie and asked if he would like to join the River Authority but he didn't wish to move and asked if I would like to do so, so I did. They were the people who look after the rivers and banks; the Broads Authority are the navigation authority. I made the move in about 1950 I think. I used to commute to Norwich. Then I was made Area Engineer for the south part of Norfolk and the north part of Suffolk, which took in the river Waveney, the Yare and the Bure. The office was in Haddiscoe by the river, near the station. So, after living in Corton for a few years we decided to live a bit nearer the office and we built a house at St.Olaves, on the top of the hill looking out over the river. Gorgeous house, lovely house, and being sited where it was it was an upside down one, we had the lounge upstairs so we had the benefit of the view. We could see Norwich Cathedral. You won't now because the trees have grown up."

As a boy, John had attended the Central Methodist Church in Lowestoft where his Father had been Superintendant – "So I spent a lot of time there and they had a gentleman name of Cattermole who was organist there. He was a school teacher and in 1941 he was evacuated with the school, so the church was without an organist. That is where I first started playing the organ in 1941/2. I played it until I joined up and when I came back I played there again. Strangely enough, during my period in the army I played on two or three occasions. I was posted to Newark and went to Newark Methodist Church and on a couple of occasions played for a service. Then I eventually got posted to Clitheroe and went to the Methodist Church where I got to know a lovely Methodist family and I played the organ there too. Only just occasionally. Anyhow, we were at St.Olaves and I used to go back to Corton to play the organ. We eventually decided this was stupid and we started going to Somerleyton Church."

So it was that John's love of the organ proved to be a boon for many churches in the area where he willingly helped out, becoming their permanent organist, not retiring until after his 90th birthday, having given over 50 years service.

"In fact forty odd years ago we installed a new organ in Somerleyton. I did all the work for it, the letter writing and so forth. It really is a magnificent instrument, it had been in Chapelfield in Norwich which was a redundant church which the city council had bought and they sold the organ for scrap for £100. We bought it and it is worth £50/£60,000 now. The one in Blundeston is a little single manual which was built in Great Yarmouth, which mechanically was perfect but not very exciting; the one at Lound was a Harrison and Harrison which is a very fine make. Lound Church was the Comper church. He was the architect who had a lot to do with the decoration of the church and the organ was part of it, the organ case was gorgeous. So as I say I eventually retired."

John's enthusiasm for the organ could lead him to talk at length about various instruments he played and knew and he found great solace in his music as he continued to play the small organ in his home. So music was a constant and important part of his whole life, as was that other passion of his – he was driving his 53rd car!

"I finished working for a living when I was 60yrs old in 1983, but I have not been idle."

Sadly John's Darling Betty became wheel-chair bound and he cared for her until her death just two months after their golden wedding anniversary. They were living in Blundeston at that time and he had no intention of moving. It was some time later that he saw the advertisement for a flat in Beccles with a window looking out over the Waveney Valley. "Out of curiosity I came over, walked in and looked out of the window and said, 'Yes I'm coming here.' So I did and that was the start of a whole new chapter, meeting a lot of new people; an interesting place for someone in my condition, this wonderful village location, shops, people and everything else and the view. I've got a house organ which I still love. It gets a lot of use but I don't play anywhere else, but I do play at home and that is good for me. I used to do a tremendous amount of walking [family holidays with their two boys were often in the Lake District], good walking you know but now I still walk, not nearly as much as I would like to but as much as I can. I've been associated with Somerleyton Church parish magazine, in fact we were editors for some time. I've always contributed to it [his latest monthly column was entitled 'View From My Window'] and helped with the distribution. I always used to finish my little bit with 'Dew you keep a troshin'. It is something which means something in my life because I am perfectly certain that I'm very lucky. I've had my health problems but I'm lucky to have got as far as I have and be as fit as I am because I've done things, I've been active, kept my body active and my mind active; I'm all in favour of that and I think that makes a lot of difference. So I still try and keep active but I find that it is not as easy as it was. I still drive and feel quite comfortable with that because I drive when I'm awake but I've made up my mind that the first sign of anything I'm going to stop – but I feel quite happy at the moment."

No wonder that those gathered for his 90th celebration felt not only affection but much admiration too.

'Dew you keep a troshin.'

ACKNOWLEDGEMENTS

My appreciation to David Woodward for his constant support and to Julia Jones for her encouragment when I most needed it. Thank you, Catherine for allowing me to use your father's drawings, he is remembered with much fondness. My thanks also to David from Edge Computers, whose help was invaluable at times of crisis, and to the team at Matador. Most of all my heartfelt thanks must go to my husband, John, not just for his not inconsiderable editorial skills, but for his forebearance in reading so many drafts.